Advanced *Conversation with Character*

By Bill & Derri Smith

A home-based language arts curriculum

Curriculum and aids for real life
sweethomepress.com

© 2006 Sweet Home Press

© 2006 Sweet Home Press

Advanced Conversation with Character

Copyright Information

Unless otherwise noted or by unintentional omission, this publication and all its parts are property of Sweet Home Press. To reprint or otherwise use content in excess of 200 words or equal to an entire page, whichever is lesser, contact us at contact@sweethomepress.com

Anecdotes appearing in italicized text without attribution represent statements of one or both authors, Bill and Derri Smith.

Scripture quotations are taken from the New American Standard Bible®, Copyright © 1960, 1962, 1963, 1968, 1971, 1972, 1973, 1975, 1977, 1995 by The Lockman Foundation. Used by permission. (www.Lockman.org)

© 2006 Sweet Home Press, all rights reserved

Sweet Home Press
sweethomepress.com

© 2006 Sweet Home Press

Advanced Conversation with Character

Table of Contents

Introduction

1. In the Beginning
2. First Impressions
3. Asking Questions: The Key to Good Conversation
4. Do Talk To Strangers
5. Written Conversation
6. Giving and Receiving Compliments
7. Introductions
8. Conducting an Interview
9. Being Interviewed
10. This Is Hard to Say: Part 1
11. This Is Hard to Say: Part 2
12. Handling Criticism
13. Public Speaking
14. Formal Occasions
15. Other Social Situations
16. Political Activism
17. Getting Closer
18. To Every Tribe and Tongue
19. Silence Is Golden
20. Conversation Do's and Dont's
21. Parting Thoughts

© 2006 Sweet Home Press

Advanced Conversation with Character

Introduction

Advanced Conversation with Character builds upon the 22 parent-led lessons in the highly-acclaimed **Conversation with Character**.

Conversation is becoming a lost art in today's culture. Families sit side-by-side watching television, teenagers can do little more than "grunt" and spouses quickly share pertinent information before falling off to an exhausted sleep. Yet relationships are, most would agree, what life is all about. And conversation is the primary tool we are given to develop those relationships past the level of business partnerships, past superficial banalities and into the deep and beautiful sharing of lives for which we long.

The goal of Christian parents is to help children relate to people as Jesus did—leading them to acquire the mind of Christ to see people as He does. Parents want children to have his heart for the unlovely, the socially inept, and the lonely, as well as for friends and family.

The Golden Rule sums up the type of conversation we desire for families. Listen the way you want to be listened to. Talk about others and to others the way you want them to talk about and to you. Consider ways to bless your conversational partner, rather than focus solely on your own interests.

As with most things, exercising good conversation skills comes down to a matter of the heart. That is why issues of character are a integral part of the study of conversation.

Words are powerful. Whether spoken without thought, or with malice or for good, every word that you speak has lasting power. The Book of Psalms describes the tongues of the evil men as swords. (Psalm 57:4 and 64:3). Likewise, "the word of God is living and active and sharper than any two-edged sword." (Hebrews

Introduction

4:12). So, no matter whether you serve yourself, the enemy or God, your mouth is armed and powerful.

When you commit to make everything you say and do a service to God, then may the Lord richly bless your conversations for the greatest good.

Advancing Beyond the Basics

Advanced Conversation with Character (ACwC) compares to **Conversation with Character** (CwC) in the following ways.

- CwC trained children in conversational basics, from answering the telephone to saying "thank-you." ACwC both builds on these basics and addresses new topics appropriate to older students.
- CwC is 22 parent-led lessons. ACwC is a 21-chapter guide for self-teaching, and therefore more suitable for older students.
- CwC ends each chapter with activity suggestions that often involve the whole family. ACwC challenges the self-learner with ways to personally put each lesson into practice.
- Both books are based on the belief that conversation is a God-given tool to be used with excellence, and that training and effort are keys to such excellence.
- Both books prominently feature Bible verses and famous quotes related to each lesson.
- Both books present good character as the essential ingredient for the exercise of conversational skill.

How to Use this Book

Who Is This Book For?

Advanced Conversation with Character is written for students ages 13 to young adult. A responsible, motivated student with a minimum junior high level reading ability should be able to work through the lessons on their own. (Optionally, this book can be used as a parent guide for instruction of one or more students.)

> **Hebrews 4:12**
>
> For the word of God is living and active and sharper than any two-edged sword.

> **Note:**
>
> When you encounter an anecdote in italics, this is the author, speaking from personal experience.

Advanced Conversation with Character

How Is This Book Used?

Using this book is very simple:
1. Read a chapter.
2. Execute the Plan of Action
3. Optionally, memorize the Bible verse and famous quote at the beginning of each chapter.

Work through the book, spending one week on shorter chapters and up to two weeks on longer chapters. Most of the student's time will be spent in the "Plan of Action," practicing skills. Working through the book at a faster pace is possible, but not recommended.

Learning can be enhanced if the student memorizes the Bible verses and quotations featured at the beginning of each chapter. For the acquisition of time-honored wisdom to incorporate into conversation, the authors recommend **Quotes with Character**, a book of 201 quotations that students copy, memorize and recite.

Be flexible to move quickly through topics the student has already mastered for their maturity level, and spend more time in areas of special interest or need.

How Should Parents Be Involved?

It is up to parents to decide the level of involvement needed to make sure the student reads the lessons, pursues the Plan of Action and, optionally, memorizes verses and quotations. Parents should encourage the student to discuss and practice conversation skills at meal times with other family members, and in life, in general. There are occasional practice activities that will need participation by parents and/or siblings. In general, though, students can use this book on their own.

Should You Start First with Conversation with Character?

In most cases, training children in the art of conversation should begin with **Conversation with Character**, but it depends on the needs of each family and student.

Students well into their teens have benefited from CwC. The family-style approach makes that basic book a lot of fun. CwC lays a solid foundation for character-led conversation. **Advanced Conversation with Character** builds on that foundation, preparing them for the adult world by honing skills, focusing on specific needs and weaknesses and equipping them for adult conversational situations.

On the other hand, a teen (or near teen) who already has a good grasp on the basics of conversation can begin with **Advanced Conversation with Character** without first using CwC.

To what do you attribute your rise to leadership in the flock?

Advanced Conversation with Character...that, and a good flea collar.

© 2006 Sweet Home Press

1 In the Beginning Was the Word...

John 1:1

In the beginning was the Word, and the Word was with God, and the Word was God.

"The time has come,"
the Walrus said,
"To talk of many things;
Of shoes and ships and sealing wax,
Of cabbages and kings."

Through the Looking Glass by Lewis Carroll

Words Are Important

When John begins his gospel with the words "In the beginning was the Word, and the Word was with God, and the Word was God," he echoes the very first words of Genesis, "In the beginning, God..." But very soon we also read, "And God said..." (Genesis 1:3)

In **Cries of the Heart**, Ravi Zacharias says, "Right from the beginning, God revealed Himself as a God who speaks. He is a communicating God, a God of reason, a God of wisdom, a God who reveals His thoughts."

As those created in the image of God, it is not surprising that scripture resounds with the importance of our words. A child is admonished to give heed to the words of his parents, and the words of parents to a child can carry blessing. Words hold potential to make our hearts glad or to stir up anger.

Word usage requires restraint. We can speak correctly or incorrectly, with knowledge or foolishness, to the right audience or to the wrong one. We can speak too quickly or too much. Our words can be true or false and carry the power of life or death, as when a judge pronounces a *sentence* (or punishment) on the guilty.

Jesus said we do not live by bread alone, but by every word that proceeds from the mouth of God. And, one day, Jesus says, people must give an accounting for every careless word. (Matthew 12:36)

© 2006 Sweet Home Press

Indeed, the Bible (Old and New Testaments) uses "word" 1222 times (New American Standard version). Clearly, words are vitally important.

Conversation Is a Key To Success

Stanford University monitored for ten years a group of Master of Business Administration graduates. What did they learn? They learned that their ability to converse had a huge impact on their success, and that grade point average had no bearing, whatsoever.

Throughout history, people rose to places of leadership and influence because they could communicate effectively and motivate others. These skills are important in most jobs, in sharing your testimony of God's work in your life, in social settings and in making and keeping friends and good family relationships.

Conversation Builds Relationships

Sometimes in America, we act like talk is just about sharing information—getting down to brass tacks, so to speak. But conversation is also about emotional connection with others. It is not unusual to find men and women approaching conversation from different angles.

Unless a man wants to convey or learn facts, he might remain silent. A woman, on the other hand, tends to recognize the relational aspect of conversation and will engage in small talk simply to engage oth-

---

Advanced Conversation with Character

Art, as Well as Science

Consider the following two statements:

1. "Hey, guys. I'd rather die than put up with more British tyranny."

2. "I know you're scared about the future but you can trust God."

Both are perfectly fine statements, and say what needs to be said. But consider the same two thoughts expressed with more artistry

1. "Give me liberty, or give me death!" -**Patrick Henry**

2. "Never be afraid to trust an unknown future to a known God."-**Corrie Ten Boom**

These statements have more power. They remain in the mind to be pondered over and recalled at **germane** moments.

People without faith develop skill of speech, as well as in other arenas. To impact the world, it behooves us to do the same.

ers. A woman might, therefore, develop closer relationships, while a man makes information sharing more efficient.

These are generalizations not true of all men and women, but observe and listen; see if this might be true among your family and friends, or maybe in yourself. A skilled conversationalist—one who rises above natural tendencies—will both cultivate the relationship and efficiently share information.

Fear Factor

A major barrier to effective conversation is fear. If you feel paralyzed when engaging in conversation, you are certainly not alone!

Fear is not all bad. Proverbs 1:7

says fear of God is the beginning of knowledge. You learn at an early age to fear or respect dangerous things, like a hot stove or a height from which you might fall. But fear can also carry a high cost. For instance, you have something important to say, but fear keeps the words from crossing your lips.

In the business world, fear limits advancement. In the community, fear keeps you from doing what needs to be done, and it stifles creativity. Fear keeps you from sharing what needs to be said and needs to be said effectively.

In the Kingdom of God, the power of fear might keep you from speaking what God has given you to speak. In every realm of life, fear can serve as bondage, blocking effective conversation.

Moses struggled with such a fear, as we read in **Exodus 4:10-11**:

"Then Moses said to the Lord, 'Please, Lord, I have never been eloquent, neither recently nor in time past, nor since You have spoken to Your servant; for I am slow of speech and slow of tongue.'

"The Lord said to him, 'Who has made man's mouth? Or who makes him mute or deaf, or seeing or blind? Is it not I, the LORD?'"

Moses feared rejection. We, too, fear rejection. The best way to tackle such fear is to decide that the risks are worth the long term benefits, and to prepare by learning and practicing conversational skills, as you will using **Advanced Conversation with Character**.

Advanced Conversation with Character

☑ Plan of Action

- ☐ Challenge yourself this week. Pick a situation that is normally a bit intimidating for you, like conversing with an adult you don't know well. Concentrate on making THEM feel valued, listened to and comfortable.

- ☐ Do a word study in the book of Proverbs, on "words" and "tongue." Write down some of the principles you glean from your reading.

- ☐ Learn how to use two new words this week, and use them in conversation. You might select words from this lesson that you may not know, like *germane*.

- ☐ Make a list of reasons to improve your communication skills. Keeping this in a place you see often will help motivate you to more effective conversation.

2 First Impressions

> **Proverbs 29:4**
>
> The voice of the LORD is powerful,
>
> The voice of the LORD is majestic.

> You never get a second chance to make a first impression.
>
> Unknown

Those First Seven Seconds

First impressions are important, and they take about seven seconds to make. When you meet someone face-to-face, 93% of how you are judged is based on non-verbal data—your appearance and your body language. Only 7% is influenced by the words you speak.

They say you can't judge a book by its cover, yet we invariably judge other people based on first impressions. When your initial encounter is over the phone, 70% of how a person perceives you is based on your tone of voice, and 30% hinges on your words. Clearly, what you say does not communicate as much as the way you say it.

Look and Act with Confidence

Eventually, looking and acting with confidence will help you *feel* more confident. Here is how:

- Stand straight.
- Look people in the eye.
- Talk loudly enough to be easily heard.
- Show up well groomed (nails trimmed, face and hands clean, hair brushed and no body odor).
- Dress neatly and appropriately, shoes shined.
- Act in a calm, dignified manner.
- Keep your hands still.
- Speak clearly, using standard English.

© 2006 Sweet Home Press

> **Advanced Conversation with Character**

- Interrupt what you are doing and stand to greet an adult who enters the room.
- Mean what you say and say what you mean, avoiding ambiguous responses like, "I guess so." If you don't know, just say you don't know. If appropriate, offer to find out the answer and report back.

But I Am Shy

Maybe you don't know what to say. Maybe you are shy. If you just stand and say nothing, people may assume you are unfriendly. Say *something*, even if it is not brilliant and witty.

Eyes Off Self

Get in the habit of flashing up a prayer, asking God to help you bless the person you will be speaking with, and to think about ways to make them feel valued and listened to and to meet their needs. What passes for shyness is often an unrecognized form of self-centeredness. When we are thinking about ourselves and the impression we are making, this feeds shyness.

Pick the Right Time

Picking the right time, when you have a choice, makes a big difference in how well your message is received. Someone who is distracted, in a hurry or irritated is less likely to respond favorably to your initial encounter. Practice with parents...

NOT when they are:

- getting in or out of the car
- rushing out the door to go somewhere
- writing a letter on the computer
- on the phone
- exhausted or sick

Surefire Ways to Make A Poor First Impression

- Slouch
- Shuffle your feet
- Slump in your seat
- Fiddle with your clothing, ears or hair
- Act hyper
- Pepper your speech with filler words (like, you know, uh) and sloppy words (yeah, nah)
- Talk only about yourself
- Complain
- Speak too quickly or too slowly

And Remember

Being late for an appointment never makes a good first impression; punctuality does.

Speak Clearly

Imagine opening a math book to the following word problem:

There were fifteen in the bag. Apples, that is. You see, this lady was going to the store. But, well, she had to run back to the car first before she started shopping. She was going to buy some things for Thanksgiving dinner. But she left her shopping bag in the car. She needed some apples and wasn't sure if there were enough for her pie recipe. Her grandmother gave her the recipe. She was going to make two pies and the recipe said she needed four large apples for each pie. So she needed to figure out if there were enough apples in the bag. How would she do that?

Frustrating, isn't it? All the needed information is in the problem, but it is presented in such a disconnected way that it is confusing and tiresome to wade through.

Here is a real life example:

Girl: Oh, they are getting scientific now.

Mother: Scientific?

Girl: Yes, about the average temperatures in the weather.

Mother: Huh?

Girl: At schoolathomesite.org!

Here is a better way to say it:

Girl: "The people at (web site) are getting scientific about the weather now; they are talking about averages."

Lack of clarity will frustrate your listeners, leaving a sour memory.

The tone of voice and emphasis on certain words changes the meaning a great deal. This can lead to misunderstandings and leave erroneous impressions in our listener's minds. Here are examples:

I'm so glad you won the game (with sarcastic tone, indicating that you are not really glad at all.)

I'm so glad you won the game. (Indicating that you didn't want someone else to win.)

I'm so glad you won the game. (Indicating that you are saying this simply as a duty— that you don't really mean it.)

I'm so glad you won the game (Indicating that you genuinely share this person's joy.)

Try these statements with differing emphasis and voice inflection:

Did you feed the dog ?

What are we having for dinner tonight?

Are we going to Aunt Matilda and Uncle Henry's house tomorrow?

Think of a few examples of your own.

Advanced Conversation with Character

Develop Clear Speech Habits

Have you ever turned off the volume on a radio or TV commercial because the car salesman was shouting or because an announcer's voice grated on your nerves?

Communication can be blocked by the way you talk: mumbling, speaking overly loudly, using a whiny voice, monotones, a sarcastic tone, a high squeaky voice, or a demanding/gruff/grating voice.

Saying Much without Speaking

In the workplace, your nonverbal communication impacts greatly what a boss thinks of you and what customers and co-workers think, too. The same is true in social settings. A person who dresses neatly and appropriately for the occasion, smiles and appears friendly and confident, reflects well on themselves before they ever say a word.

☑ Plan of Action

- ☐ Consider the things you've learned in this chapter, and ask close friends and/or family members what your weak points are. Then ask them to gently point it out to you each time you repeat a mistake.

  Perhaps you can work out a secret signal. This will increase your awareness level. Or simply have them report to you after a social encounter with others. You may be surprised to hear how many times your bad habit emerges. Eventually, you will be aware that you are about to complain, (or whatever habit you are working on) BEFORE you do it and it will no longer be a habit.

- ☐ Work on developing a pleasant, clear tone of voice in many ways. Record yourself reading a speech, part of a play, a poem or a story, and listen critically. Try rereading the same piece, working each time to improve clarity of speech and voice intonation.

- ☐ If you tend to mumble, practice exaggerating the pronunciation of words and confidently projecting your voice.

- ☐ Listen to and, when possible, observe speeches by excellent communicators. Note body language, use of pauses, tone of voice and inflections.

You will make an impression on someone today. It is just a matter of which kind.

© 2006 Sweet Home Press

3 Asking Questions: The Key to Good Conversation

Did you ever notice how enjoyable it is to talk about yourself? This chapter helps you grant that joy to others, as well as deepen relationships.

Make Others More Important Than Yourself

People like it when you seem to want to know them. They find it charming, and you gain influence. Dale Carnegie, author of the well known book, **How to Win Friends and Influence People,** tells of a conversation with a potential business client. The prospect talked for two hours. Carnegie actively listened, saying only about two sentences. At the end of the conversation, the prospect told Carnegie he was the best conversationalist he had ever met, and he bought Carnegie's product.

Through humility, Dale Carnegie exerted influence over a buying decision by exhibiting genuine interest in knowing the client.

This chapter prepares you to ask the questions that fuel good conversation and increase communication.

With children your own age, ask about interests, school studies, hobbies, favorite books, music, people you know in common (avoiding gossip and rumors), places traveled, movies, relatives, pets and so forth.

When talking to adults, ask about the work they do, experiences they had when they were younger, places they have traveled or

---

Philippians 2:3

Do nothing from selfishness or empty conceit, but with humility of mind regard one another as more important than yourselves.

Who questions much, shall learn much, and retain much.

Francis Bacon

Advanced Conversation with Character

about their hobbies and interests.

Be alert to visual clues. If you visit someone's home or office, you will find many items to ask about, like travel souvenirs, family photographs and books.

Be Prepared

Have a few standby questions prepared, in case no other topics come to mind, like "What is the nicest thing that happened to you today?" Prepared questions can sound a bit artificial, but asking them can help keep a good conversation flowing.

Choose Questions Carefully

Unfortunately, not every question is appropriate.

Questions with Implied Criticism

Consider your motivation for asking a question. Consider, too, how a question might be perceived. Is your question actually a criticism? Imagine giving a gift and then hearing the recipient ask, "Where am I supposed to put *that*?" The message comes through loud and clear. They don't like the gift.

Consider how these questions might come across:

- "Don't you even have a computer?" (This question implies the other person is lacking because they do not have the same possessions, and it promotes discontentment.)

- "Don't you know that Consumer Reports rated that brand the very worst?" (This question implies, "You certainly are foolish buying that brand.")

The Question Game
(2 players at a time)

One player picks a theme and asks an open-ended question (not one that can be answered "yes" or "no"). The other player responds with a related open-ended question. Play continues back and forth as long as the players can continue without repeating a previous question or making a statement.

This game can also be played in a group, with each person asking a question based on the one before.

Example:
Theme: Food

- Why is it important for people to have food?

- Where does our food come from?

- What would happen if there were no food?

- Is food important for other purposes than feeding people?

- What professions require a knowledge of food?

3 Asking Questions

- "Can you believe Jane wore a dress above her knees?" (This question presumes the other person has the same standards as you, and it reveals more negative aspects of your own character than of Jane's knees—judgmentalism, love of gossip and disregard for Jane. Your friend might wonder what you say about THEM when they are not around.)

Money Matters

Don't ask how much something cost or talk about the cost of something you or your family has.

Approach Beliefs with Caution

Questions that seek to reveal common beliefs and values, whether religious, political or otherwise, can quickly strengthen a new relationship, as will be discussed in the chapter *Getting Closer*. Unfortunately, questions that expose differences can quickly end that same relationship. Even if the purpose of your conversation is to better know someone, proceed understanding the potential consequences of ill-timed or ill-chosen questions.

For example, friends might agree on many things, but feel differently about whether there should be more laws regulating gun ownership. You might have a thorough and healthy discussion on the matter. If, however, your father owns several guns, uses them often and your family believes there are too many restrictions on guns, then you must guard against overstating your family's opinions. Your verbal crusade against gun regulation might rub your friend very much the wrong way.

In this example, tread carefully if your friend or their family has had bad experiences with guns. Perhaps someone was shot or injured in a gun accident.

There are times and places for a healthy and vigorous debate, but choosing those times and places well preserves relationships and honors your friend.

Let Them Answer, Let Them Ask

Having multiple questions in mind is good, but avoid overwhelming your conversational partner with a non-stop barrage. He might feel more like he is being interrogated than befriended!

Remember, too, that conversation is like a game of catch, where you toss the ball back and forth. It is not like golf, where the same person keeps hitting the same ball. Give your partner a chance to ask some questions, too, and/or offer a bit of personal information before you ask another question.

The old adage of many a teacher says, "There is no such thing as a stupid question." Never make the other person feel foolish for asking something by answering in a condescending way. Instead, appreciate the person's humility and desire to learn something

Advanced Conversation with Character

new; those are admirable traits!

The most important part of asking questions is to slow down and listen to the answers. When you carefully listen and observe (emphasis, pitch, body language, etc.) you discover what they value. Then you know what is important to them and can hone in on those subjects.

When, for example, your conversational partner tells you a fact, like what their job is, their major in school or a special hobby, ask them what it is that got them interested in that.

If you don't have much information to go on, ask where they are from, then ask how that place is different from where you are now. If they have always lived in the same place, ask why they like it. Go from facts to thoughts, feelings and opinions. (More on this in the chapter *Getting Closer*.)

☑ Plan of Action

- ☐ Play the Question Game, explained earlier in the chapter.

- ☐ Who makes you feel special? Who seems able to get to know you better than most people? The next time you are together, pay attention to the types of questions they ask, and see what you can learn.

- ☐ Note places in the New Testament where Jesus asked questions. See if you can detect his motives in doing so, and note the reactions of the people he questions. The answers to Jesus' questions were not always painless, but they always led to something good. For starters, try Mark chapter 9, verses 33 through 37.

Avoid self-serving questions, like those in...

The Prayer of the Cat

Lord,
I am the cat.

It is not, exactly, that I have something to ask of You!

No-
I ask nothing of anyone-

But-
if You have by some chance, in some celestial barn,
a little white mouse,
or a saucer of milk,
I know someone who would relish them.

Wouldn't You like someday to put a curse on the whole race of dogs?

If so I should say,
Amen

From **Prayers from the Ark** by Carmen Bernos de Gasztold, translated from the French by Rumer Godden. English edition published 1963 by Macmillan and Company Ltd. London, Toronto and New York.

4 Do Talk to Strangers

Matthew 25:35

"For I was hungry, and you gave Me something to eat;
I was thirsty, and you gave Me something to drink;
I was a stranger, and you invited Me in..."

Many a friendship is lost for lack of speaking

Aristotle

I strolled the airport terminal, awaiting departure home to Nashville. Passing the newsstand, I thought it curious to see a woman crouched behind a magazine rack frantically paging through a popular celebrity gossip magazine as if both wanting and yet fearful of finding bad news. I didn't get a good look behind those sunglasses, but I thought I recognized this woman's face.

I later boarded my flight and watched as the same lady from the newsstand came down the aisle and sat in front of me. This time, I got a better look. She was a very famous country music star, who immediately leaned back with her head turned toward the window, pretending to sleep. The woman sitting next to her made all the signs of wanting to be friendly, but had no response from this seemingly fearful celebrity who did not want to be noticed.

It is doubtful anyone could have pried this lady out of her shell that day, but we do well to be prepared when it is the right time to talk to strangers. It could be that this lady really needed to talk, but was afraid.

The basics of beginning a conversation were covered in **Conversation with Character**. Here we take a deeper look at ways to start a conversation with someone you don't know. First, note that it is understood here that it is not always a good idea to strike up a conversation with a stranger. Allow parents to train and guide you in avoiding dangers. Beyond that, here is advice on how to proceed.

© 2006 Sweet Home Press

Advanced Conversation with Character

Go Prospecting

You may have had the occasion to note how unsatisfactory it is talking to a person who does not want to have a conversation. Perhaps you missed some clues. Note if a person's attention is focused on a task or other inputs (radio, music, telephone, etc.). Or do they look up and smile when you enter? If so, then they are probably interested in talking with you and would enjoy meeting someone new.

This is your cue to make eye contact, smile back, and speak! You don't have to start off with a wonderfully witty remark; if they are interested in talking, they will likely give you a bit of information about themselves that you can use as a springboard for more personal conversation.

Take a Little Risk

Avoiding all risk and all possibility for failure leads to a life impoverished of, among other things, rich relationships. You may avoid failure, but you will neither achieve success nor experience the satisfaction that success brings!

Besides, you ARE making a decision by NOT making a decision. If you are in a group of strangers, for example, and you don't decide to start up a conversation with someone, they will likely conclude that you are not interested in doing so and not interested in THEM.

At the Right Moment

Some always wait for "just the right moment" and never find it. Something will always be wrong (too tired, forgot to brush teeth, in a hurry, unable to think of a really clever opening line or whatever—always.

Take Intelligent Risks

The ability to take intelligent risks is a large determining factor in a person's level of achievement. For every reasonable risk, there is the potential for some reward that would not be reached by staying in one's comfort zone.

Here are a few ideas for taking healthy risks, to broaden your body, mind and spirit. Plus, developing new interests is a great way to meet new friends!

- Take a class to learn something new.
- Start a collection.
- Make friends with people completely different from you (older, another nationality, etc.).
- Sign up for a race and train for it (walk, run, swim, bike).
- Volunteer in your community.
- Do something each day just to please God, that no one else will know you did.

© 2006 Sweet Home Press

That's the way life is.) If you are in a crowd and thinking about starting up a conversation with someone who is not otherwise engaged, just do it!

Note: It is generally appropriate for men to speak to men (boys to boys), and for women to speak to women (girls to girls).

Use Questions and Opinions

It's usually best to open a conversion with a question or an opinion. If you simply state a fact, this leaves the burden on the other person to think of a question or opinion or to simply drop the "conversation" with no more than a nod or smile. "Great meeting!" or "It's really cold today," are two examples of fact-based openings. Here are some better alternatives:

Find a Springboard Topic

Ask about something you are interested in or confused about, preferably something the other person might be interested in, too, and/or know something about. This will get the conversation started. Then you can listen carefully to whatever information the other person shares, and use that to springboard into further discussion.

Examples:

- At a club meeting: "What do you know about the leader?" or "What made you decide to join this club?"

  At the store: "I see that you bought Thai noodles. I've always wondered what you can make using them."

- If at Jeremiah Tousend Park: "I wonder who Jeremiah Tousend is?"

You don't have to use these openers or anything like them. Anything like this will work just as well. Just open the door!

Talk about the Person

Observe carefully. Note the other person's clothing, what they are saying or doing. Find something you are interested in knowing more about. People like talking about themselves! It is usually best not to start by talking about yourself.

Examples:

- To a boy with a scouting uniform on: "I've been thinking about joining the scouts. How would I go about doing that?" Or "What do you enjoy about scouting?"

- At a 4-H meeting: "That is such

© 2006 Sweet Home Press

Advanced Conversation with Character

an interesting display about the Parelli method of horse training. What are some methods you have found to be effective? Why?

Form a Friendship

Take the initiative! If both you and a friend (or potential friend) wait to suggest you do something together or otherwise show that you are interested in getting to know each other better, guess what—it will not happen!

It might be best to start by suggesting something that doesn't require much time or effort, like, "Would you like to get a Coke at that diner across the street?" Such a suggestion to someone you just met and would like to know better, is more appropriate than, "Want to go camping with me and my family next weekend?" Take friendships one deliberate step at a time, and practice the language of building relationships.

Be specific. Don't say, "I'd like to take a walk at the park with you sometime." A well-known similar phrase among adults who only pretend to seek friendship is "Let's do lunch sometime."

If you want to propose a specific activity together on Sunday, don't first ask, "Are you doing anything next Sunday afternoon?" That is awkward for the other person. Maybe they have no plans. But maybe they don't really want to make plans. Once they hear what you are asking, they will not have a very graceful way of declining the offer.

It may embarrass them to say they have no plans, as it is like saying, "I don't have anything to do, because I have no friends." To avoid embarrassment, they may say "Yes, I have plans."

It is best to be direct: "Would you like to (activity) with me (or with my family) at (time, date and place)?"

☑ Plan of Action

- ☐ Make it a point to talk to at least two strangers this week, putting these ideas into practice.

- ☐ Role play giving an oral invitation. Have a parent or other knowledgeable person offer suggestions for improvement.

© 2006 Sweet Home Press

5 Written Conversation

Proverbs 17:27

He who restrains his words has knowledge, and he who has a cool spirit is a man of understanding.

In times like the present, men should utter nothing for which they would not willingly be responsible through time and in eternity.

Abraham Lincoln

I recall an older, and usually wiser, man commenting on our new computer—the first computer in the neighborhood I might add—and remarking that this was another fad that would come and go. He is probably correct, but that was 26 years ago, and I think this computer fad has a few more years before it goes out of style. (I should probably send him an email to see if he remembers that comment.)

In 1990, we got an email address. It was pretty exciting at first. Then we realized that we knew only two other people in the world who also had email, and they didn't write much.

So many fads do come and go, but computers have held on to revolutionize the way we communicate in writing.

Much of the information in this book applies to written as well as spoken communication. Especially in the 21st century world of electronic communication, written and verbal conversation often intertwine. This chapter explores a few basics of written conversation.

Written Words Are Weightier

Written communication is a permanent record that may be read by anyone, whether you intend it or not. While verbal expression can be recorded in audio form, it is normally heard only by the person(s) present when the words are spoken. While it is always impossible take spoken words

© 2006 Sweet Home Press

back from the ears that heard them, written words may last and be read by generations to come.

Just as a written contracts overrule verbal agreements in court, written words carry greater weight in society than spoken words. Therefore, it is important to modify conversation style when it happens in writing.

Show Your Style

Tone of voice and body language shape conversations. Spelling, punctuation, grammar and word usage, whether rightly or wrongly employed, shape written communication. How well you use these shaping tools communicates to the reader your education level, intelligence, expertise and reliability. For this reason, style manuals, such as **The Elements of Style**, by Strunk and White, are well worth studying and keeping nearby as a reference.

Make Computers Work *For* You

Computers are wonderful writing tools. Words, sentences and paragraphs can be rearranged easily. Corrections are made with a few keystrokes. Spelling and grammar checks help minimize errors. Here are some electronic communication tips:

Word Processor

If you are experienced with a computer application like Microsoft™ Word that checks spelling and grammar, then you know not to **relay** on the computer as the final word on spelling and grammar. (Oops! See, we told you!)

Take a little time to learn how to use the dictionary and thesaurus functions available on computers. The little time spent learning

---

Advanced Conversation with Character

Emoticons and Acronyms

Following are abbreviated expressions commonly used in informal email and online chats:

Emoticons

:) or :-)	Happy
:D or :-D	Laughing
:(or :-(	Sad
:Q or :-Q	Confused
:O or :-O	Surprised
:-&	Tongue-tied
:-/	Perplexed
;-)	Wink or Kidding

Acronyms

BFN	bye for now
BTW	by the way
FYI	for your information
FWIW	for what it's worth
HTH	hope this helps
IMO	in my opinion
IMHO	in my humble opinion
LOL	laugh out loud
ROFL	rolling on floor laughing
TIA	thanks in advance
VBG	very big grin

will serve your writing for years. In the end, however, it is a good idea, especially for an important written communication, to have someone more experienced and knowledgeable (like your parents) look it over for errors.

Email

Like words that travel from the gut directly off the end of the tongue, without first filtering through the brain, email messages are so easy to send that many people click send too soon. By heeding these tips, you are less likely to regret that last email:

- Make the subject heading short, but informative. The subject, "John Smith" leaves the reader guessing. Is he dead or running for election? Did he move to China? Are we clarifying that it's John Smith rather than Bill Smith? The subject, "Birthday card for John Smith" makes things much clearer.

- Don't use all capital letters in email. It is equivalent to shouting, and it is harder to read.

- Before placing confidential information in an email, consider this: It might be forwarded to someone else, even accidentally. Even years from now, the files might be found and read.

- Emoticons, like ☺ or :) are fine for letters to friends, but are not appropriate for more formal correspondence, like to a business or school.

- Make paragraphs shorter than you would in print, and don't indent. Double-space between paragraphs for readability.

- Lacking body language, tone of voice and facial expressions, it is all too easy to be misunderstood or offensive using email. Before you click "Send," review your message and consider how it could be misunderstood.

- Double-check the address field before you send. You may embarrass yourself by sending the message to the wrong person, not to speak of causing offense.

- Anyone who uses email much knows that some messages don't get through to the intended recipient. Allow for the possibility someone will not receive your message. Follow up by some other means, if you don't hear back.

Advanced Conversation with Character

Heed These Tips for All Written Communication

- Be clear and concise. If you can say everything that needs saying in three words, don't settle for four or five. Edit, and then edit again.

- Avoid slang.

- In general, it is best not to use abbreviations or symbols, such as ampersands (&), in place of words.

- Be sure to spell names correctly.

- In business letters, it is wise to provide a quick overview of the issue. Busy people do not appreciate needing to read to the end of a letter to discover how it pertains to them.

- Use 10 to 12 point size for the main body of text. A 14 to 20 point font is best for main headings, bold or normal. Sub-headings are normally 10 to 12 point bold. (This text is 12 point.)

- *Italics* and **bold** are more difficult to read than regular font. That is why it is used sparingly in the main body of text.

- Main headlines should be shorter than 15 words

- Sans serif fonts (like the Verdana Ref font on this page) have a more modern look than serif (like Times New Roman).

- Avoid fancy fonts and graphics or pictures behind text that make words difficult to read.

- For business and other non-personal letters, the rule of thumb is that your letter must be read and understood in less than 20 seconds, or its chances of success are limited.

- Remember that effective written communication means enabling your reader to clearly understand your meaning, in as few words as possible.

☑ Plan of Action

- ☐ Keeping the *Tips for Written Communication* in mind, write a practice letter to a business, asking about an order that has not arrived. Have an adult look it over and tell you how you did.

- ☐ Write a letter to a family member who you do not often see, like a grandparent or cousin. Choose someone you think might write back.

- ☐ If you already use email, look back over your last five messages. How well do you follow the advice in the chapter? Work on improving your electronic communication.

6 Giving and Receiving Compliments

> **Proverbs 27:2**
>
> Let another praise you, and not your own mouth;
> A stranger, and not your own lips.

> A compliment is a gift, not to be thrown away carelessly, unless you want to hurt the giver.
>
> Eleanor Hamilton

Corrie ten Boom (20th century Christian speaker and author of **The Hiding Place**) was once asked how she avoided pride in the face of many compliments and the praise that was showered upon her. She replied that she looked at each compliment as a beautiful long-stemmed flower given to her. She smelled it for a moment and then put it into a vase with the others. Each night, just before retiring, she took the beautiful bouquet and handed it to God, saying, "Thank You, Lord, for letting me smell the flowers; they all belong to You."

Conversation with Character covers the basics of Giving and Receiving Compliments. Here, we delve into more detail.

Receiving Compliments

When you receive a compliment, respond with a smile and a "thank-you." To do otherwise, makes the other person feel they said the wrong thing. The right way is so simple, it hardly needs a whole chapter to explain. It is the wrong ways to receive compliments that easily fill the pages of this chapter.

When someone compliments your dress and you simply say, "Oh, this old thing?" or they tell you that you sing well, and you say, "Oh, no. I really am not good at all," you sound ungracious.

Such comments can also be taken as your

© 2006 Sweet Home Press

attempt to coax even more compliments and further reassurances. Besides, if you turn away, deny what they say or change the subject abruptly, you aren't likely to receive many more compliments from THAT person!

Is There an Echo in Here?

Try to avoid returning the same compliment that has been given to you. It seems like a perfunctory comment made just to be nice:

Example: "I like your purse."
Answer: "I like your purse too."

Giving Compliments

When offering compliments to others, be sincere. If a person even suspects that you do not mean what you say, they will not receive well this or future compliments.

Third Person Compliments

Some of the most valuable compliments are those given third person. Speak favorably about a person who is within earshot of a conversation or tell someone who is likely to pass to another what you said about them. Return the favor by passing on to others the compliments you hear about them.

Now, here is a special tip that helps some people through their awkwardness at receiving a second-hand compliment: Follow up with a related question.

Example: "My friend is in your ballet class and she tells me that you show great promise as a dancer. She saw you in the Nutcracker and thought you were the best ever in the role of Clara. How did you become interested in ballet?" or "What did you do to train?"

The follow-up question puts the person at

Advanced Conversation with Character

Priming the Pump

Here are some compliment ideas to get you started:

You
- are a terrific leader.
- are so good at building people up
- are really reliable
- are so creative.
- are a good provider.
- are fun to be with.
- have an excellent reputation.
- are perceptive.
- make a house feel like a home.
- are a good driver; I feel safe with you.
- are a good listener.
- have a great outlook on life.
- are kind.
- are a good role model.
- are so funny
- sure are strong
- are courageous.
- are loving.
- really bring out the best in me.
- are a wonderful cook.

ease and gives them something to say other than, "Duh, I'm speechless."

Indirect Compliments

Indirect compliments are some of the most believable and therefore cherished.

Examples:

- Asking for advice shows that you value a person's judgment
- Asking questions, listening with great concentration, making eye contact and making another feel you have nothing better to do than listen to them; these make a person feel significant.
- Remembering to offer birthday greetings shows you value a person.
- Telling a person you want to spend time just with them—and doing it—is a compliment to that person. An afternoon at the park after a comment like that, will help a person feel cherished. You could have done many things with your time, but wanted most of all to be with them

Remember: Compliments are sincere. Flattery is not. Compliments are meant to benefit the receiver; flattery is designed to benefit the giver.

Bring Out the Best with Compliments

Have you ever noticed that you are at your best with people who think the best of you? Thinking and speaking well of others helps them to be their best.

If you praise a person's generosity, he will become more generous; if you praise a person's trustworthiness, she will become more trustworthy; if you praise a person's kindness, he will become more kind.

Our words have great power to build people up ... or tear them down. Let's use that power well!

© 2006 Sweet Home Press

> **Advanced Conversation with Character**

☑ Plan of Action

Play Games

- ☐ Consider involving younger children in these games, teaching them how to give and receive compliments.

  - Each player writes all the other family member names in a vertical list. Then write a true compliment for each letter of the person's name.

  - Toss a ball or beanbag to a family member, stating something positive about them. The receiver then throws the ball to someone else and compliments them. Continue for a specified period of time.

  - Write the letters of the word "Compliments," one letter to an index card. Each time a family member receives a compliment from those outside the immediate family, they earn a letter. Once all the letters to the word have been earned, celebrate with a special privilege: (a family movie or game night, a pizza delivery, special treats...)

Seek Wisdom

- ☐ Search the Bible for insights about flattery and its consequences. Look also for passages that tell about thinking the best of others and building others up with our speech. Memorize one or more verses, and meditate on it this week.

7 Introductions

Leviticus 19:32

You shall rise up before the grayheaded and honor the aged, and you shall revere your God; I am the LORD.

There are two types of people - those who come into a room and say, "Well, here I am!" and those who come in and say, "Ah, there you are."

Frederick L. Collins

Imagine that you are Jim Smith, who has just agreed to say a few words at a convention of 2,000 people in a downtown hotel ballroom. And, now the introduction begins:

"Ladies and gentlemen, the programs committee asked me to introduce to this assembly one of the most interesting and accomplished journalists of our time.

He reported from the very tent on the Iraqi sands where the American general accepted Iraq's surrender in the first Gulf War. He has since written best selling biographies of several world leaders who he personally knew and spent considerable time with.

"I'm sure I speak for us all when I say that we come here today with great excitement to hear from George Hoyt, journalist, and writer extraordinaire.

"Unfortunately, Mr. Hoyt had a last minute change of plans. Instead, I now turn the microphone over to Jim Smith."

The story above might give you a sense of just how awkward an introduction can be—how you might feel when poorly introduced. This chapter provides you an introduction to introductions, from personal one-on-one introductions to introducing a speaker to a gathered throng.

The Personal Introduction

Introductions sometimes happen when you least expect them, so get ready, get set, go! If you're not already standing, stand up

Advanced Conversation with Character

for an introduction. Make eye contact; no staring into space or studying your shoes. Smile!

If you are introduced to someone and you do not hear the name clearly, simply ask them their name. If you have previously been introduced to someone, do not assume they will remember you or your name. Saying, "Hi, John. I'm Mary. It's good to see you again" helps avoid an awkward moment for the other person.

Rebound from a Forgotten Name

Everyone forgets a name. Try introducing the person whose name you do remember and hopefully the other person will chime in with their name. If not, choose the best wording. By saying, "I've forgotten your name," you imply that the person wasn't worth remembering. However, if you admit to forgetfulness with, "I've just drawn a blank," or "My memory seems to be malfunctioning," you avoid embarrassing or insulting the other person. Let the blame be your memory and not the other person's personality.

If you can't remember someone's name, but you remember an interesting point about them, cite it. You might say, "I clearly remember our conversation about Thai food, but your name seems to have temporarily slipped my mind. Please help me out." Then get off the subject of the memory lapse and onto something more interesting to everyone.

Help avoid this problem by repeating the name when you first hear it ("It's nice to meet you, Sam") Not only do you project a genuine interest by repeating their name, but the repetition is more likely to imprint the name in your memory.

Introducing Yourself to a Group

There are many group settings in which you may need to provide your own introduction.

Here are some tips for introducing yourself to a group:

- Make it brief and memorable.
- Give the information about yourself that those present would find interesting.
- Smile.
- Don't forget to tell your name.

Have a memory hook; something in your introduction that so vividly describes what you do or who you are, that people will be able to visualize it clearly in their mind's eye. It doesn't have to be funny, but that helps.

Example: "Did you ever want to shoot a relative? Call me, I'm a photographer!"

© 2006 Sweet Home Press

7 Introductions

When someone seems to have forgotten your name, just jump in, a smile on your face, and offer your name.

Get Your Act(ions) Together

It is customary for the following to occur during introductions:

Men—When introduced to a man or woman, a man rises if he is seated. He shakes hands with another man when being introduced but traditionally waits for a woman to extend her hand before offering his.

Women—Should remain standing until the elderly or senior woman is seated. A woman does not usually rise when introduced to a man. The younger or junior woman usually waits for the older or senior woman to offer her hand. A woman customarily extends her hand first to a man.

Provide Conversational Kindling

It is helpful to include enough information about all parties to an introduction so people know how to get a conversation going. This information is like kindling to a campfire. Examples:

"Mrs. Robertson, this is my cousin, Mary Horne. Mary, Mrs. Robertson is my music teacher."

"George, I'd like you to meet my friend Micah. We're in boy scouts together. Micah, George lives two houses down from me."

Use Correct Name and Title

It is helpful to introduce people by the name they should be called. For example, introduce adults to children by titles like "Mr." or "Mrs."

When you meet or make introductions at an event (like a club or conference), you help the conversation along by mentioning your connection to the organization or a mutual interest that brought you there. For example:

"Gina tells me you participate in *Communicators for Christ* training. I am interested in debate. How has the *Communicators for Christ* organization helped you?"

Speak to the Higher Ranking Person First

A good rule of thumb is to use the formal name of the senior person when making an introduction so that the junior person isn't placed in the awkward position of only knowing a senior person's first name. For instance, when introducing your boss to your younger brother, you wouldn't say, "Bob, I'd like you to meet my brother, Billy. Billy, this is Bob, my boss." Instead, say, "Billy, this is Mr. Greengate, my boss."

Here are some other examples:

"Mr. President, this is my father, Mr. Roberts."

"Mrs. Jones (customer), this is Mrs. Hines, our store manager."

(The manager will want you to give preference to the customer.)

"Grandma, this is Mrs. Anderson." (Older person outranks younger.)

"Dr. Richards, may I introduce my mother, Mrs. Armstrong?" (An untitled person is usually introduced to a titled person)

If two people are of equal position, it doesn't matter who you introduce first though it makes sense to introduce the one you were speaking to at the time to the person who arrives.

Introduce the Speaker

Prior to a speech, have the speaker supply you background information, and ask how he or she prefers to be introduced. Learn the correct pronunciation of their name. Keep the introduction short, but enthusiastic.

Don't undermine the speaker by talking so much about the topic yourself that you give part of the presentation. State the exact title of the speech and share why the topic is of interest to the audience.

A pause and gesture toward the speaker before giving his or her name and title directs audience attention to the speaker.

Finally, ask the audience to join you in welcoming the speaker, and begin the applause.

Make the introduction short, and make it count.

☑ Plan of Action

☐ If you have a younger sibling, teach them the basics of making introductions. Then have them bring a stuffed animal to the table and introduce it to the family!

☐ Write an introduction for one or both of the following speakers Keep the introduction to 30 to 45 seconds.

- A homeschooled student, winner of a national spelling bee, who will be telling the secrets of her success

- A well-known person, speaking on state legislation that affects the rights of traditional families.

© 2006 Sweet Home Press

8 Conducting an Interview

Proverbs 16:23

The heart of the wise instructs his mouth and adds persuasiveness to his lips.

Give me six hours to chop down a tree and I will spend the first four sharpening the axe.

Abraham Lincoln

As a teenager, I benefited from the kind attention and hard work of a church youth leader who was in his early 50's. I knew this man and had great respect for him. Or did I? Ten years later, I found myself interviewing this same person to come work for me. I knew Mitch as a youth leader, but I knew very little about his employment history and job skills. What would my boss think if I hired a friend who wasn't right for the job? What would my former youth leader think if I didn't hire him? Would Mitch get the job done right, and, in any case, how could I tell from an interview.

This chapter prepares you to conduct an interview. Once you understand the job of an interviewer, the next chapter will prepare you for the "hot seat," as interviewee.

Conducting an interview is like riding a horse. Some horses are half dead, taking you nowhere; some are mostly wild, taking you where you didn't expect. Whether you are a news reporter, a researcher, an employer or in some other capacity as an interviewer, you often don't know how responsive your interviewee will be until the interview gets underway. And there may be surprises, too. Best to prepare now for your adventure as an interviewer.

Preparing for the Interview

Who will you interview? That is the question that needs more than simply a person's name for an answer. The more you know ahead of time about the person you will

© 2006 Sweet Home Press

Advanced Conversation with Character

interview, the better use you can make of your interview time.

Getting to Know the Interviewee

The most common ways to learn about your interviewee are to read what they say about themselves and what others say about them. Search the news. Search the Internet. Call people who know them or who have talked to them. If you are conducting a job interview, carefully study the interviewee's application or resume. If you plan to interview someone you already know, then you have an advantage. You will be better able to focus on the important questions.

What Is the Objective?

What is the objective of the interview? Some interviews are really just a listening service. You may have occasion to "interview" someone who has lived a very long time. Such people have much to tell about life, and your willingness to ask one or two questions and then sit and listen accomplishes a possible objective of the interview—to perform a service for a person who needs to be heard. (Hopefully, you will gain wisdom and knowledge from the experience, as well.)

The purpose of an interview with a librarian might be to learn about library science. Or it might be to learn how to become a librarian. Maybe the purpose is to learn more about literature or about the benefits and working conditions of a librarian. Attempting to cover all of the above in one interview may be too ambitious. It is best to identify the objective before you get there.

Right out of college, I was a newspaper reporter. One day I had an opportunity to meet and briefly speak with Bob Hope, a

Job Interviewer Ground Rules

A job interviewer is faced with enough written rules to keep two attorneys busy round the clock (or so it sometimes seems).

Among common rules are:

- Don't ask a woman if she plans to have children. (Some employers don't want to hire a woman who plans to be off having babies. In the U.S., it is illegal to base hiring decisions on such factors, and asking the question can mean legal trouble for the employer.)

- For similar reasons, don't ask questions about or make comments about a person's race, age or religion.

- Don't ask if a person was ever arrested (in most states you may ask whether they have been convicted).

The potential pitfalls for an interviewer are numerous. It takes practice and training to avoid them all AND to accomplish the objective of filling a job vacancy with the right candidate.

8 Conducting an Interview

Sample Questions

Here are questions you might ask of someone who knows about a field of work that interests you.

- What do you do on a typical day?
- What training or education is required for this type of work?
- What part of this job do you find most satisfying? Most challenging?
- Which professional journals and organizations would help me learn more about this field?
- What personal qualities or abilities are important to being successful in this job?
- Is this type of work in demand?
- Do you have any suggestions for me on how to best prepare for this type of work?
- How did you get started?

very famous 20th century entertainer. All I could think of was how great it would be to meet this person who was so well loved by the American public. Like I said, that was all I could think of, and when I finally shook Mr. Hope's hand, my little reporter's notebook dangled to my side. I asked him every question I had prepared: None! I was virtually speechless. The comedian's eyes quickly sized me up for the star struck fan I was—the sort he encounters every day. He said a polite "good-bye" and walked back into his dressing room.

Researching a Career

While interviews are most commonly associated with the hiring process, a wise young person might interview people who have knowledge of the field in which they hope to find work.

Emily DeRocco, Assistant Secretary for Employment and Training with the Department of Labor in the George W. Bush administration, was asked for advice from a 17-year-old homeschooler named Holly. Holly asked what she could be doing to prepare for a future job as a librarian, besides her volunteer library work. Ms. DeRocco replied, "It sounds as if you are focused on a goal, Holly, and you are doing some of the right things by reading and volunteering … One of the best things you can do is talk to librarian...find out what skills you need to gain in order to be successful."

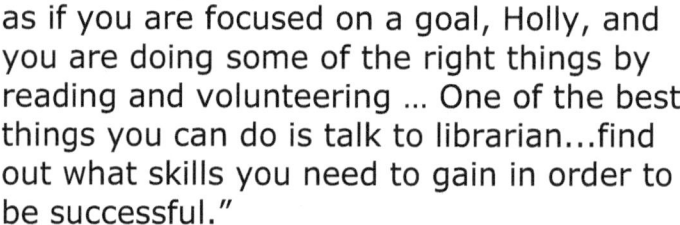

Great advice! In this case, YOU will be the interviewer. Here are some tips for that role.

© 2006 Sweet Home Press

Advanced Conversation with Character

Identify Possible Interviewees

If, for example, you want to interview people who work a field that interests you, start with lists of people you already know: friends, fellow students, present or former co-workers, supervisors, neighbors, etc.

Contact a professional organization in the field of your interest. Ask someone at a college career center or alumni office for a list of people working in that field. Consider people your parents know.

Don't be timid. People generally like to help students with job information. Contact the person to set up an interview. Depending on the situation, that may mean writing a letter and following up with a telephone call or having a mutual acquaintance make the contact for you.

Come prepared with a list of possible questions. Mark the ones you want to be sure to ask, and use the others as time allows. Don't let your list keep you from listening, engaging in conversation and asking for additional information.

Ask open ended questions, like "Tell me about a typical day in your work?" for "What do you like about your work?"

At the end, ask for names of others who might be helpful to you, and ask permission to use their name when contacting these new people. This a process is called "networking."

☑ Plan of Action

☐ Practice by interviewing your family members.

- Schedule a time to interview each person, getting their permission. Think of something each person knows more about or can do better than you (and, where siblings are concerned, take with you an extra dose of humility). Even younger siblings have the experience of being a unique person. Maybe you have forgotten some of the finer points of caring for dollies <wink>.

- Now that you have selected interviewees, decide what your objective is for each interview. Write possible questions, and place star next to the most important questions.

- When you conduct the interview, make sure there are no distractions, like loud music or prior commitments (like chores undone).

- Take notes so you can recall later what you learned. End the interview when your purpose is accomplished.

9 Being Interviewed

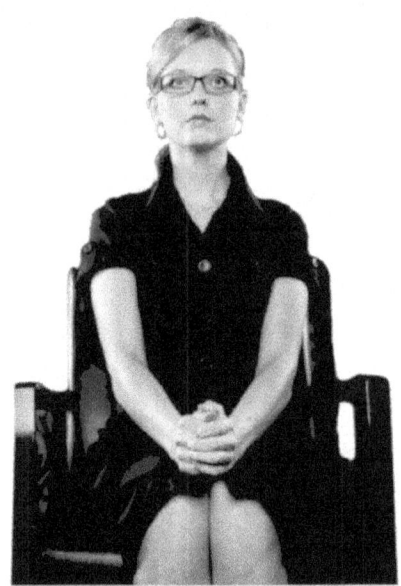

Now that you know something about the interviewer's side of the conference table (or *kitchen table* in your practice sessions), you know a bit more of what the interviewer expects from you as the *interviewee*.

This chapter helps you prepare specifically for the job interview and the college interview, but much of the advice applies to other interview situations.

Keep Your Eye On the Objective

You learned in the last chapter that the interviewer has an objective. You should know what that overall objective is. If you don't, then ask before you accept the interview appointment. You, too, have an objective, whether to get a job, get accepted in a school or win a scholarship.

Make a list of everything you can truthfully say that helps fulfill both the interviewer's objective and your own—like experience, education, skill and interests. If any of this information is complicated or difficult to explain (like why you didn't go to college), then practice how to say it in the most positive and concise way.

The Job Interview

Let's start right in with a list of basic do's and don'ts for a job interview. Many of these tips apply equally to other interview situations:

Psalm 141:3

Set a guard, O LORD, over my mouth; keep watch over the door of my lips.

Never wear a backward baseball cap to an interview unless applying for the job of umpire.

Dan Zevlin

© 2006 Sweet Home Press

Advanced Conversation with Character

- Don't be late...don't be late....don't be late. Be 15 minutes early.

- Don't repeatedly respond with only "yes" or "no."

- No gum (no lollipops, no corncob pipes).

- Dress well: It is better to be overdressed than too casual. Be immaculately groomed. Polish your shoes. Dress conservatively and get rid of anything unconventional (color streaks in the hair, body piercing jewelry, etc.)

- Don't eat foods that will leave odor on your breath (like onions or garlic).

- Be alert and interested. Lean forward and listen attentively. Keep good eye contact. Show enthusiasm and be as diplomatic and congenial as possible

- Be sure you understand each question. Ask for clarification, if needed, then answer concisely.

- Be honest. Don't claim to have skills or expertise that you don't. Not only is it dishonest, but it could lead to a short and painful time in the wrong job.

- Avoid slang. This is not the time for "Awesome man," "Yeah, like...," "Totally rad," or "This company really rocks!"

- Be interested in the interviewer. Notice some small thing about him—perhaps a picture or a collection in his office—and ask about it. Be genuinely interested in his responses...and show it.

- If a shortcoming becomes apparent, admit it but don't be self-effacing. If the interviewer says "You're very young" say something like this: "Yes, I am seven-

Frequent Job Interview Questions

- Tell me about yourself.

- What kind of work do you want to do? Why? When did you decide this?

- What are your strengths? Your weaknesses?

- Tell me about a time you had conflict with another person and how you resolved it.

- What is your GPA? (grade point average)

- How much money do you want? Would you work for less?

- Tell me about a situation where you had to persuade another person to your point of view.

- What do you want to be doing in five years?

- What is the biggest challenge you have faced?

- Are you available to work extra hours?

- How would you handle an irate customer?

© 2006 Sweet Home Press

teen, but I think you will find me mature for my age."

- Respond only to what is asked; don't volunteer information that is not relevant or which might cast doubt on your abilities.

- Try to put everything you say in a positive light. Rather than going on about why you left the last job so quickly, say "I don't have a lot of experience, but I think you'll find me a good worker, and, if you give me a chance, I know I can do the job."

- Never criticize a previous employer, and never complain (about the weather, the forms you had to fill out, etc.)

Open-Ended Questions

Sometimes, an interviewer will just say, "Tell me about yourself." This is not the time for your life story. Remember the list you made of things to say that accomplish the objective.

The interviewer will often ask if you have questions, especially toward the end of the interview. Have some questions prepared. This is your chance to see if you really want to work for this person or company. You might ask about the company vision, details about the job, possibilities for advancement, what the employer is looking for in a candidate and/or who the people are that you'd be working with.

Be Willing to Lose the Job

Your objective should not be so rigid that you are not willing to lose a job opportunity. Do your best, but don't exaggerate your qualifications. Walk into an interview seeking the very best outcome, even if that means working someplace else.

College Interviews

A college interview is a good opportunity for the admissions officer to get to know you as a person, beyond what your grades and test scores tell him.

A standard interview usually lasts 30 minutes to one hour. Arrive early to allow time to find the office you are going to (most colleges are a maze of buildings). Ask in advance where you may park. Upon arrival, ask the receptionist the name of the interviewer so you will pronounce it correctly when you actually meet him/her.

Advanced Conversation with Character

Be polite to the receptionist and other staff you encounter.

If possible, learn who will interview you before hand, and read about him in the school catalog or on their website. Then you can say something that shows your interest and resourcefulness, like, "I noticed in the catalog that you went to the same college as my father (or whatever)." Show some interest in their accomplishments.

Study the school catalog and any other materials about the college before the interview. You don't project a positive image if you ask questions that a careful reading should already answer.

Prepare well, and rehearse the points you want to make, but don't memorize the words. You don't want to come across as having a canned speech. You want to appear natural and spontaneous.

Remember that every question you are asked is an attempt to see if/why the college should accept you. Try to answer that question in every reply you give.

Come prepared with intelligent answers to standard questions, like those listed to the right.

Handling the Hard Questions

In answering questions about a failure, remember that everyone makes mistakes. Admit failure, then quickly move on to tell what you learned from it and how you worked to ensure that it would not happen again. The interviewer wants to see that you can handle failures and learn from them. Never be rude or challenging.

Not much can make up for overall poor grades, but they may be ok if:

Frequent College Interview Questions

- How would your friends describe you?
- What else should I know about you?
- What's your favorite subject in school? Why?
- What extra-curricular activities have you participated in?.
- What have you done that you are most proud of? Why?
- How do you get along with people?
- Why do you want to attend this college?
- Why should we accept you?
- Have you had any leadership roles? Tell me about them.
- What's the last book you read?
- What job experience do you have? (Note: don't forget applicable volunteer jobs, leadership positions in organizations etc. It doesn't have to be a job for pay.)

9 Being Interviewed

Bad Impressions, Without Saying a Word

Consider the impressions made by each of these non-verbal clues.

- **Slouching** (lazy or won't make a good impression on customers)
- **Arriving Late** ("I'm unreliable" or "Your time is not important to me.")
- **Looking Out the Window** (doesn't have good people skills, has something to hide or not interested in the job)
- **Aroma** ("doesn't bathe often" or "That after-shave will drive away customers.")
- **Touching or covering part of face, biting pens, fidgeting, playing with hair, etc.** (nervousness, lack of confidence)
- **Either "Limp fish" or bone crushing handshake** (I'm not sure I'm going to like this person)
- **Hands behind head** (too relaxed or too informal)

- They are concentrated in a particular subject ("I'm a great student, but Math is my biggest challenge.")
- They are confined to a particular period of time. ("I had a prolonged illness," or "I was working three jobs and was too busy.").

Try to gracefully move the conversation on to something positive, pointing out your stronger grades and/or improvements after a difficult period.

Your Turn to Ask Questions

College interviewers often end an interview by asking if you have questions. You do not want to ask basic questions that were clearly answered in the interview, so don't just memorize a question ahead of time.

Have a few categories of questions in mind and fine-tune the question to cover something not already addressed. Here are a few possibilities:

- What kinds of educational and vocational placement services are available to students?
- Are there educational opportunities off campus, such as courses at neighboring colleges, study abroad, or internships for people with your desired major?
- Are there opportunities to volunteer for community service?
- (If the interviewer is an alumni) What did you especially like about your college experience?

Advanced Conversation with Character

After Any Interview

Immediately write the interviewer a short note, thanking them for their time and reemphasizing your interest in the position. Get it to them as quickly as possible, preferably before the end of the following business day. Standard mail is still a common option, but use of quicker communication channels, like electronic mail, is growing as the standard replacement for the postal service. Use email if the option is available. The quicker your message arrives, the greater likelihood you'll reinforce a positive impression.

Do make sure your message or letter contains correct spelling and grammar. A poorly worded follow-up message can be worse than none at all. Have an adult look it over.

If you interviewed with several people, don't just change the name at the top of the letter. Individualize each one. Your note can actually work against you if there are two or three duplicates collected together in your file.

☑ Plan of Action

- ☐ Have someone interview you. Tell them what their objective is. Make it a topic in which they have expertise. For instance, your mother might interview you to determine if you have the aptitude and desire to be the family's full time dishwasher. (You can pretend on the "desire" part, if necessary.) This is a great opportunity to practice the principles presented in this chapter. Ask for constructive feedback to guide you toward improvement.

For more of a "real life" experience, find a family friend who interviews people in their job. Ask them for a practice interview. The more practice you get, the better prepared you will be for some of life's major turning points (jobs, college admission, etc.).

© 2006 Sweet Home Press

10 This is Hard to Say—Part 1

How did you handle that last argument? How are you feeling about it? This chapter prepares you to disagree without being disagreeable.

Disagreements

Conflict is a part of every person's life. It is not avoiding conflict that enables you to navigate life and conversations, but rather it is the ability to engage and satisfactorily resolve those conflicts which cannot be avoided.

Remember these things when you have a conflict in your relationships:

Do not discount another person's feelings. Listen carefully. Accept the other person's right to feel as they do. Say, for example: "So, when I am late, it makes you really angry, and you feel that I don't respect your time. Is that it?"

You may not agree with the other person's assessment and you may have valid reasons for being late, but a respectful response like the one above shows that you heard the other person and understand their feelings. Don't water this understanding down by defending your actions. Avoid denying their feelings by telling them they will be okay, they are just overreacting, they need to cheer up or that they are being illogical. Those things may be true, but blurting it out makes ultimate conflict resolution all the more difficult.

Remember, by acknowledging a person's

Romans 12:18

If possible, so far as it depends on you, be at peace with all men so that it may be well with you, and that you may live long on the earth.

Fallacies do not cease to be fallacies because they become fashions.

G. K. Chesterton

© 2006 Sweet Home Press

Advanced Conversation with Character

feelings or perspective in this way, you are not saying they are right. You are not surrendering your side of the story.

Stay calm and in control of your emotions. This shows respect for the other person, keeps the conflict from escalating and usually earns you respect. Proverbs 26:20 says, "For lack of wood the fire goes out."

Clearly and concisely state the problem from your viewpoint. "When you do THIS, THIS is the effect, and it makes me feel like THIS." Example: "When you leave your toys all over our room, I have to clean them up or trip over them, and I feel embarrassed when friends visit. That makes me annoyed." You needn't repeat this, unless the other person clearly misunderstands you.

Remain factual. Don't add your interpretations ("You just do that to bug me.") Don't attack the other person or call names ("You're such a slob.") Talk about their actions. Don't generalize ("You ALWAYS leave your things wherever they fall.") Keep in mind that *love is not arrogant or rude*.

Keep the conversation on the topic at hand. Don't replay every wrong that has been done to you by this person. *Love does not keep a list of wrongs.* Be willing to compromise for the sake of love. *Love does not insist on its own way.*

Corrections and Contradictions

Most of the errors people make in conversation are trivial. If someone gets a name or a date wrong, or mixes up other minor details or mispronounces a word, it is not worth correcting that person and embarrassing them for such a minor point, especially in the presence of others.

Pressure Points

Even "friends" may try to manipulate you into doing something you don't want to do or that is wrong or harmful. Here are common tactics to watch for, as well as possible responses.

- **Put-Down**
  Example: *You're just a sissy* Possible reply: *I know what is important to me, and this doesn't fit.*

- **False** *information*
  Example: *Smoking cigarettes makes you so cool!* Possible reply: *Having lung cancer is not my idea of cool (or having nicotine stained fingers or having stinky smoke breath).*

- **Threat of rejection**
  Example: *If you don't do this, I won't be your friend any more.* Possible reply: *A real friend won't ask this of me.*

- **Threat of embarrassment.** Example: *EVERYONE is doing this. Possible* reply: *I never wanted to be everyone.*

© 2006 Sweet Home Press

If the error is major and needs to be addressed, do it in private, and allow the person to "save face." Make the correction with humility and respectfulness. It is better, for example, to approach the issue as if you might have misunderstood. Besides, if it turns out you are wrong, it could actually save you embarrassment.

You might say, "I was taught that the Civil War was between the North and the South. Perhaps you are right that it WAS between the French speaking and English-speaking Canadians, but let's look it up." Give the other party a chance to say, "Well, now that you mention it, I might have been wrong about that." This defuses anger, embarrassment and bitterness.

If *you* made the mistake, don't prolong the interruption by replaying why you might have thought that or how you might be right under different circumstances. Even if you humbly accept that you are wrong, don't tarnish your humility with prolonged expressions of regret. That just makes you the center of attention at the expense of others.

Times to Speak Up

There are times in clear issues of right and wrong or defending someone's reputation, when you may be free to speak up, even if an adult has said something clearly wrong. Be polite and respectful, but speak up if it is appropriate and needed. Examples:

Prejudice: "All (Blacks, Poles, Chinese, Mexicans...fill in the blank) are (lazy, greedy, dishonest, etc.) Possible answer: "Mr. Jones, I was taught and have observed myself that there are good and bad people in every culture. My friend's family is from Poland, and they are amazingly industrious. They came to this country with nothing and they've build up a business of their own."

Honor: "Senator Green is a liar." "Mr. Brown, Senator Green is my uncle and I know him to be a truthful and honorable man." (He will probably think before he makes such a statement again. Oh, and don't say he is your uncle unless he really is.)

If an adult is present who addresses such controversies, it is best for you to remain quiet. It is better for adults to deal with correcting other adults.

Correcting Poor Manners

It is not your job to train others or to monitor their manners. It is your job to be trained by your parents and to watch your own manners. There may be occasions with a very close friend where you would gently mention a problem area. Best

Advanced Conversation with Character

policy: Ask your parents whether it would be appropriate to say anything at all.

You Made a Mistake

Be honest and accept responsibility without rationalizing or offering excuses. You will be more respected and appreciated in the end.

Will Rogers was talking to a radio announcer about to make his debut who said, "I'm petrified. What if I make a mistake?" "Go ahead and make one!" Rogers said with a smile, "It will make people think you're almost as human as they are."

Everyone makes mistakes. There isn't much you can do when you have said to your new friend, " New Yorkers are so rude," and then learn her family is from New York. Just say something like, "I'm sorry, I seem to have a talent for saying the wrong thing. Please forgive me." Then move on.

☑ Plan of Action

- ☐ Make a "list of wrongs"—the things people around you often say that annoy you. Then tear the list up and throw it away. Consciously choose to overlook trivial mistakes in family conversations this week; your lips are sealed!

- ☐ When areas of disagreement arise with your siblings, parents or others this week, put the steps you learned in this chapter into practice. Notice the results. See if your efforts result in an improvement in relationships.

- ☐ Humble yourself, and ask someone you are close to if your responses communicated to them respect and value. Ask if there are ways you can improve. Then act on those suggestions. You'll be on the way to maturity!

Tact and Courtesy

"Don't flatter yourself that friendship authorizes you to say disagreeable things to your intimates. The nearer you come into relation with a person, the more necessary do tact and courtesy become.

"Except in cases of necessity, which are rare, leave your friend to learn unpleasant things from his enemies; they are ready enough to tell them."

Oliver Wendell Holmes (1809 - 1894), **The Autocrat of the Breakfast Table, 1858.**

When conflict goes awry, treat the affected area before infection sets in.

© 2006 Sweet Home Press

11 This is Hard to Say—Part 2

Proverbs 25:20

Like one who takes off a garment on a cold day, or like vinegar on soda, is he who sings songs to a troubled heart.

The nature of bad news infects the teller

William Shakespeare

Adults are often called upon to deliver news that will be unpleasant to the hearer. Such bad news may range from telling a friend that her stream of forwarded emails is unwelcome to telling someone you will not be inviting them to your party, firing an employee or notifying parents that their military son died on the battlefield.

Delivering Bad News

Tell the truth. It is the right thing to do, and people respond better when they understand a situation.

Be clear. Anticipate questions and answer them. Think "who, what, when, where and why." Don't leave people guessing about your meaning. Imagine a doctor being misunderstood when he says, "We lost your aunt." Better to be clear: "Your aunt died."

Respect people's feelings. It is not unusual that people receiving bad news respond with some emotion. Don't say, "It's not that bad," or "Don't worry," or otherwise disregard the feelings of the one to whom you deliver bad news. Nor is this is not the time for light-hearted comments. Show respect for the other person, saying, for example, "I know this is frustrating" or "You must be worried/angry/scared/upset/hurt," etc. Try to imagine yourself in a similar situation and how you might feel. Treat others as you would like to be treated.

In person or in writing? Some things are well dealt with in writing, but more personal

© 2006 Sweet Home Press

Advanced Conversation with Character

issues need to be dealt with in person, or at the very least on the telephone. Imagine the damage that can occur when a boss sends an e-mail telling a person they are fired. Worse yet, that the employee would learn of it for the first time on the company bulletin board.

Make eye contact. Eye contact helps to assure the hearer that what you say is true, and that this news is important.

Pick the place. Find a private spot to break bad news. Some experts say a room with subdued colors, lighting and acoustics calms the emotions of the person receiving the bad news.

Allow time for any questions and concerns. Don't pick a time when you are in a rush, especially when bad news may be taken personally, as a rejection.

Here is how the conversation might flow:

1. "I appreciate your kind invitation for me to speak to the Youth Group."

Explain in a positive and tactful tone the reasons you cannot accept.

2. "I am already committed to pick up my grandparents at the airport at that time."

Next, break the bad news.

3. "Therefore I will not be able to attend the luncheon on Thursday afternoon."

Or you might decide to switch the order of steps 2 and 3, as it seems to suit the situation. Offer alternatives, if possible, to help the other person meet their goals—like the name of another qualified speaker they can ask or an alternative meeting time.

Gracious Ways to Say "No"

- **The short and sweet "no":** "I hate saying 'no' to you, but I really must this time." or "No, thanks."

- **The 'priorities" no:** My priorities right now are very few and focused. I won't be able to squeeze this one in.

- **The 'too busy" no:** What a wonderful invitation - but I'm just stretched too much to accept it."

- **The SHORT explanation 'no':** "No, I'm helping my dad paint that day."

- **A partial no:** " I can't spend the day stuffing envelopes but I can come from 10:00 to 12:00.

- **A 'leaving the door open for the future" no:** " Oh, I wish that I could baby-sit tomorrow. I always have a great time with your children! But I'm sorry ☐- I just can't."

- **The "not me" no:** " That's not really something I enjoy." Or "That's not for me, thanks."

© 2006 Sweet Home Press

You Goofed

You forgot a friend's birthday party, missed an appointment or broke a window. Don't lie, make excuses or blame someone else.

The sooner you confess, the better. Tell whoever needs to be told, and take responsibility for your actions. Say that you know it's your fault, how sorry you are, how awful you feel and, if appropriate, ask if there is anything you can do to make amends.

Better yet, make amends on your own if it is clear how that can be accomplished. For example, if you missed a friend's party after saying you would come, send a note restating your regrets. Send a small gift to show that he/she is important to you.

Accidents and Awkward Moments

Like it or not, everyone spills drinks, drops food or knocks over a lamp at some point. A sincere "I'm so sorry," or "Please forgive me," is always in order.

Do all you can to help clean up a mess. Offer to replace or repair anything you've damaged. And make sure to follow through.

If you simply bump into someone without any real harm done, a simple "I'm sorry," or "How clumsy of me," will suffice.

Once you have appropriately dealt with the mistake, don't dwell on it. Move on.

Saying "No"

Don't feel compelled to offer an explanation which may encourage the other person to argue your point. Rather than telling a salesperson, "I don't have enough money," for example, try a simple "Thanks for your help. This is not what I'm looking for," or "I want to look more before I decide," or just plain "No, thanks."

The same holds true for other situations, like requests to serve on a committee, teach a Sunday School class, baby-sit or attend a meeting, for example. These are all good things, but they may not be the right priorities for you.

You do not need to defend yourself. A simple "I appreciate you asking me, but I'll have to decline" is sufficient in most cases.

One truthful way to decline taking a survey on the telephone is to say, "I'm sorry, this is not a good use of my time right now."

© 2006 Sweet Home Press

Advanced Conversation with Character

☑ Plan of Action

☐ Role-play the following situations. Humbly accept suggestions from others on how you can improve:

- A close friend wants you to come to her birthday party but you have a scheduling conflict and feel the other event is where you need to be.
- You borrowed the family car, ran over a nail and got a flat.
- You left your Science book outside in the rain, up in the tree house where you last worked on an assignment.
- Your neighbor asks you to work mowing their lawn during the summer, but you don't have the time.
- You said you would meet a friend for lunch in the park and then completely forgot about it. She waited for you and finally called to see if you were alright.
- You've been asked to play the piano for the upcoming homeschool association's play. You are completing your high school requirements and researching and applying to a few colleges, and it is a very busy time for you, so you feel you cannot make the commitment.
- You are visiting a friend's house for the first time. You bang into a family photo, knocking it off the table and breaking the glass.

☐ Write a letter explaining why you have decided not to accept a job offer. Have it critiqued by at least one and preferably two adults.

Good News / Bad News

Like coating a bitter pill with sugar, they say it is good to deliver some good news along with the bad. This philosophy has spawned many good news/bad news jokes, offered here just for fun.

Doctor: I have good news and I have bad news. Which do you want first?

Patient (bravely): Give me the bad news first.

Doctor: You are going to die.

Patient (shocked): That's awful, what's the good news?

Doctor: Not for a long, long time.

Master to Roman galley slaves who have been rowing for hours: I bring you good news. You may have 15 minutes to rest.

Crew: Fantastico! Bravo!

Master: Now for the bad news. At the end of the rest period, the captain wants to go water-skiing.

© 2006 Sweet Home Press

12 Handling Criticism and Advice

When the prophet Nathan confronted King David concerning the king's sin, David responded like this:

> Be gracious to me, O God, according to Your lovingkindness;
>
> According to the greatness of Your compassion, blot out my transgressions.
>
> Wash me thoroughly from my iniquity
>
> And cleanse me from my sin.
>
> For I know my transgressions,
>
> And my sin is ever before me.
>
> Against You, You only, I have sinned
>
> And done what is evil in Your sight,
>
> So that You are justified when You speak
>
> And blameless when You judge.

With the sort of spirit that David had, consider the advice of this chapter, which helps you receive criticism in humility, for your own ultimate good.

Proverbs 9:9

Give instruction to a wise man, and he will be yet wiser: teach a just man, and he will increase in learning.

He has a right to criticize, who has a heart to help.

Abraham Lincoln

© 2006 Sweet Home Press

Advanced Conversation with Character

When Someone Criticizes You

Humility versus pride is one of life's greatest battles. When pride has the advantage, responses to criticism go something like this:

- Ignore it.
- Change the subject.
- Go silent.
- Run and hide (perhaps slamming the door on the way).
- Answer with criticism of the other person.
- Simply deny that the problem exists.
- Make excuses.

(Just raise your hand if you recognize yourself in any of this.)

Keep Defensiveness in Check

Resisting the temptation to punch the person who criticizes is a noble beginning. Remember that the person delivering the criticism usually just wants to be heard and to have their objections taken seriously. Someone close to you may need reassurance that you love and accept them, even when they are critical. The responses listed above only deepen the conflict, and so the tension just builds.

Handling criticism without defensiveness has tremendous benefits. Rather than causing further harm, you may learn something of value—there is usually at least a grain of truth in criticisms, even those from enemies.

Try to understand what is really bothering the other person. Criticism is often stated in

Proverbs to the Wise

Pride only breeds quarrels, but wisdom is found in those who take advice. Proverbs. 13:10

The way of a fool seems right to him, but a wise man listens to advice. Proverbs 12:15

Pride only breeds quarrels, but wisdom is found in those who take advice. Proverbs 13:10

A rebuke impresses a man of discernment more than a hundred lashes a fool. Proverbs 17:10

He who scorns instruction will pay for it, but he who respects a command is rewarded. Proverbs 13:13

Instruct a wise man and he will be wiser still; teach a righteous man and he will add to his learning. Proverbs 9:9

He who ignores discipline despises himself, but whoever heeds correction gains understanding. Proverbs 15:32

© 2006 Sweet Home Press

general terms. Calmly and respectfully ask for specifics. If you can think of some yourself, ask "Is this an example of what you mean?"

Here is an example:

Mother: You are such a slob!

Daughter: What would you like me to do differently, Mom? (Asking for specifics.)

Mother: Well, I like to feel that guests can stop by at any time, and the house will be presentable.

Daughter: Are you thinking of the time when Grandma stopped by last week, and I had dishes all over the kitchen because I was baking a cake?

Mother: No. That wasn't so bad. Everyone understands having dishes out when you are cooking.

Daughter: Oh, you mean like this morning, when the neighbors stopped by with tomatoes from their garden, and my muddy boots and dirty socks were right inside the door?

Mother: Yes. That was really embarrassing to me.

This conversation shows respect for the mother's feelings, keeps a small matter from escalating into a larger one, and it lets the daughter know specifically how her mother was feeling and what she could do about it.

Agree with What Is True

Once you are able to identify the real issue, stand ready then to agree with the criticism. Even humble agreement on a part of the complaint is a step in the right direction.

Let's look at possible conclusions to the Mother-Daughter conversation. Which of the following responses is likely to result in a stronger relationship and a better informed daughter?

Mother: You tracked mud all over the house from the bottom of your boots. That makes so much extra work.

Response A:

Daughter: Well, don't ask me to weed the garden if you don't want mud in the house. It's muddy out there.

Response B:

Daughter: You're right, mom. I'm sorry. Next time I work in the garden, I'll scrape my boots on the boot scraper by the door.

If you agreed that Response B is by far the best, then you have obtained wisdom!

Say You Are Sorry

Not only did the daughter admit there was truth in her mother's statement, she also said, "I am

Advanced Conversation with Character

sorry." Many groundbreaking conversations fail for unwillingness to say those three little words, and mean them—"I am sorry." It is a conversation that fails not for lack of knowledge or skill. Rather, the tragedy is the fruit of pride.

Admitting you did something and yet failing to say you are sorry is worse than failure to admit wrong. It says, "I did it wrong, and I plan to do it the same way again."

Learn to say and mean, "I am sorry."

Do Something About It

Next, the daughter made her mother's joy complete by assuring her that, next time, she would scrape the mud off her boots before entering the house.

Now, the mother knows she was heard. She hears those powerful words, "I am sorry," and then she hears something like music that sets her mind at rest that the matter is resolved—the daughter assures her that next time she will scrape off her boots.

Now, only one thing can rob the joy and make the next occasion for criticism more painful. That would be if the daughter, after telling her mother she would next time scrape her boots, instead brings her muddy boots into the house.

Not all criticism is from a parent to child. There may be situations where you don't believe you can change future behavior (for whatever reason). If that is the case, then it is far better to be honest and say you are not ready or able to change than to lose a person's trust by failing to keep your word.

At least let the person know that you heard them and understood their concerns, even if they cannot expect a change in your actions.

☑ Plan of Action

The action comes the next time you have an opportunity to respond to criticism.

☐ In the meantime, read the 51st Psalm to get a renewed sense of true humility. Meditate on these words, so that they become a part of you.

☐ Next time you receive criticism, go through the steps outlined in this chapter:
- Listen.
- Don't be defensive.
- Admit the truth.
- Humbly say you are sorry.
- Tell what you will do next time.
- Do what you say.

© 2006 Sweet Home Press

13 Public Speaking

Proverbs 22:11

He who loves purity of heart and whose speech is gracious, the king is his friend.

By failing to prepare you are preparing to fail.

Benjamin Franklin

Public speaking may not seem to you like a conversation. Yet, many public speakers rely upon audience feedback to chart and tune the course of their message.

Virtually everyone in the Kingdom of God needs public speaking skills. Faithfully carrying God's message requires clear and effectively communication. As an adult, you may need to speak in a business or church meeting, teach, stand up for a righteous causes in the legislature or speak to the news media, to name a few examples.

Tips for Great Speechmaking

- Choose a topic you know something about and that *moves* you. If you speak about things that are important to you—things you really believe in—then your conviction and sincerity will make you a more effective speaker.

- Dress professionally and conservatively. Wear something you know you look good in (this is not the time to try out a new outfit or hairdo). Arrive early, review your remarks, comb your hair, and use the bathroom if needed.

- Walk to the front in a confident manner. Stand up straight. Wait about 3 seconds after you stand in place and face your audience before you begin speaking. Allow the same amount of time after you are done before you leave the speaking platform. This pause conveys confidence to the audience.

© 2006 Sweet Home Press

Advanced Conversation with Character

- Don't say you are nervous, even if you are.

- Remember that your purpose is not to show people what a good speaker you are. It is to change them, to present information in a way they understand, to convince them of something and/or to move the audience to take action. Concentrate, then, on your message and not on yourself.

- Be creative. Anecdotes, startling facts and/or information that relates to your audience makes your talk come alive.

- Involve the audience: For example, ask one of the audience members a question. (You will hold the entire audience's attention as they mentally respond and compare their answer to that given by the one person you asked). E.g., "Let's examine today the current state of immigration and the melting pot that is America. Mary, do you have parents, grandparents or great-grandparents who were immigrants?" (If not, then ask someone born in the United States who is not a Native American!) Inviting audience participation makes a connection with the audience and fosters a "this is about us" feeling. Alternately, have the audience do something: Ask for a show of hands or ask them to visualize a mental picture that you describe.

- Use props if applicable. For example, pass out slices of homemade bread if bread is your topic, or, if you talk is about sewing, have someone model a garment you made and point out some of its features.

- Gain credibility quickly by using testimonies, quotations, statistics, experience and/or examples.

Off To a Great Start

Grab audience attention in the first couple of sentences. Here are some ways to do it:

- **A powerful quotation**

- **A rhetorical question:** This is a question posed to get the audience thinking.

- **A startling statement:** "Did you know that Americans buy 2.7 billion packages of breakfast cereal each year. If laid end to end, the empty boxes from one year's consumption would stretch to the moon and back."

- **Illustrations:** Ronald Reagan, known as a superb public speaker, famously made his points and drew audience attention by telling stories about everyday people.

- **A commonality** "Were you ever frustrated because you could barely understand a customer service representative?"

13 Public Speaking

- Never talk longer than your allotted time. Time yourself during practice to establish the right pace and amount of content. There is almost always a way to say the same thing with fewer words.

- Be clear and concrete. Avoid vague ideas, rambling sentences and large words when smaller ones make the point. Don't be like Owl of Winnie-the-Pooh fame, who *"...went on and on, using longer and longer words, until at last he came back to where he started."*

- If you must simply write out a speech and read it, take care not to lapse into a monotone. Try instead writing key words on cue cards to remind you what you want to cover in your talk.

- Cue cards can also be used for sending messages to yourself, such as, "Slow down" or "Pause."

- Whether you have the entire speech in front of you or you use cue cards, practice enough that you can then look at your audience through most of the speech and yet not lose track of where you are. Use a highlighter to emphasize main points and words to emphasize. Put vertical marks at places where you should pause. If you speak with a full written text in front of you, leave blank space between your sentences; triple space makes the text easy to read and follow.

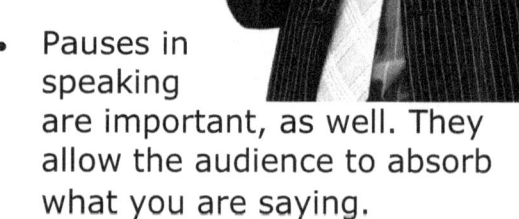

- Pauses in speaking are important, as well. They allow the audience to absorb what you are saying.

- Use eye contact. Think of your audience as individuals, which they are. Sweep the room slowly with your eyes, stopping to look for a short time at various members of the audience. Speak as if speaking to that individual. Make this contact with as many as possible. This sort of connecting with the audience helps keep you energized and enthusiastic as you speak.

- Change your position and posture from time to time. Stand awhile. Then move around a bit. Don't pace back and forth like a caged animal, but use movement judiciously to heighten interest. Vary your tone of voice, also.

© 2006 Sweet Home Press

Advanced Conversation with Character

- The best speakers sound as if they are having a conversation with the audience. Conversational tone makes the atmosphere more intimate and helps to build a good relationship between the speaker and their audience.

- Standing up straight not only makes you look more confident, it allows space for your lungs to more easily fill. Full breaths of air enable you to project your voice and vary tone appropriately.

- Use gestures naturally. A frozen, rigid stance does not convey confidence.

- Avoid objects (like a pen) with which your fingers might nervously play, thereby distracting your audience.

- A smile helps both you and your audience relax. The audience will usually smile back, and you will immediately build positive rapport. If you feel very nervous and think you might forget, write a note to yourself on your cue card to smile at appropriate times.

- If you make a mistake, just continue on as if you didn't. If a fact must be corrected for accuracy, make the correction in a matter-of-fact way, and then go on. You want your audience to feel that you are competent and that what you have to say is important to them. This will not be the case if you freeze, get a deer-in the-headlights look, stammer, stop to apologize or hang your head.

- Original humor is good if you have that bent, but avoid using commonly heard jokes unless you have a creative new twist that is relevant to your topic.

- Speak slowly. When we are nervous, we tend to speak quickly, so it takes a conscious effort to slow down.

- Close by summarizing your main points. Try to leave your listeners with a powerful illustration, quote or statement. Issue a challenge or appeal.

- If you give out handouts, do it at a time when you can look at them together or you may lose audience as they read it.

Speaking To a Hostile Audience

Some audiences have already decided they don't like you. They don't like who or what you stand for.

One way to soften them up to be more receptive to you is to begin by establishing some common ground. After all, you are all human, and there are plenty of things all humans have in common. Otherwise, the audience may be so clouded with negative thoughts that they will just naturally tend to disagree with everything you say.

Once you establish, perhaps to audience surprise, that you have common ground, they may start think "Maybe our viewpoints are not so different after all." They may be more willing to listen to your ideas—or at least not throw you out.

Try asking a series of questions to which you are sure the audience will mentally answer "Yes." This gets them thinking in a positive way and develops rapport. Example: "Do you believe in freedom of speech for all Americans?" or "Do you want your child to have the best education possible?"

Stage Fright

You have sweaty palms, a racing pulse, and a dry mouth. Fortunately your ailment is never fatal: you have a case of stage fright. Everyone is different, but possible treatments include:

- Be well prepared and practiced, with organized notes. Memorize your opening so well you could say it in your sleep.
- Pick an outfit and shoes that are flattering, appropriate and **comfortable.**
- Arrive early—but not SO early you have a long wait.
- Check your appearance in a mirror
- Breath deeply, slowly and evenly for several minutes. Consciously relax your face muscles
- Avoid caffeine and heavy meals beforehand.

A certain amount of nervousness is helpful,. The surge of adrenaline gives you focus and energy to do your best. Most people calm down once the speech starts.

© 2006 Sweet Home Press

> **Advanced Conversation with Character**

☑ Plan of Action

Public speaking is an art and a science that takes time, effort and dedication to develop. If you are serious about learning to be an effective public speaker, you will want to spend extra time completing the plan of action. This chapter and this action plan are just the beginning to what can be years of progressive levels of achievement.

- ☐ Start a file of stories and quotes. Review what you have and add to it regularly. Use this file when you need an example to support a point you are making or to begin or end your speech effectively.

- ☐ Look for opportunities to practice public speaking. Consider joining *Toastmasters*, attend a *Communicators for Christ* * training conference, join a speech club or give a testimony at church. Gaining experience will help combat nervousness, as will thorough preparation for each speech. Short of making a speech, become accustomed to public speaking by volunteering to read the announcements.

- ☐ Practice, practice, practice. Practice reading aloud or reciting Shakespeare. Practice projecting to a spot far from you. Practice speaking while the chest and shoulders stay steady and only the abdomen and diaphragm move.

- ☐ Consider taping practice sessions and listen to them. Have someone in the family give you feedback.

- ☐ Have someone video tape you giving your speech, if possible, to see if you stand stiff like a toy soldier. If so, practice using hand motions with larger movements than feel comfortable. After doing this a number of times, practice again doing what feels natural to you. Often you will have reached the correct level of movement. Video tape again to reevaluate.

---

*Check the Communicators for Christ training opportunities and resources for debate and public speaking at www.communicatorsforchrist.com.

© 2006 Sweet Home Press

14 Formal Occasions

> **Proverbs 25:11**
>
> Like apples of gold in settings of silver is a word spoken in right circumstances.

> Good manners will open doors that the best education cannot.
>
> Clarence Thomas

America is an increasingly casual society, and formal manners are out of place in most places. However, when a formal occasion *does* arise, a few basic common-sense tips will help you prepare. You will be more at ease and thus better able to concentrate on the conversations that form and maintain important relationships, rather than on which fork to use.

Many books and Web sites offer excellent guides on the use of silverware, how to properly remove your outer garments when you arrive, how to escort a lady into the room (and how to be escorted into the room), differences in practice among various cultures and nearly anything else you might need to know for even the most formal state occasion. Such research is oh so much more helpful if done before, rather than after, the event. It is beyond the scope of this book to focus on such matters. Instead, we offer conversation related tips for these special occasions.

Weddings

Few events are remembered quite like the formal wedding. Here are tips on how to be remembered for the right reasons at the traditional American wedding:

After the ceremony, a receiving line usually forms to greet the bride and groom, their parents and sometimes their attendants. Go to the first person in line, who is typically the bride's mother. Shake hands. If she

© 2006 Sweet Home Press

Advanced Conversation with Character

does not know you, or if you are not *sure* she remembers you, introduce yourself with a brief identification: "I'm Sue Smith from Connie's quilting class." Then add one more sentence about the occasion, like "What a lovely wedding." Continue down the line in the same manner, omitting introductions with people you know well. Be brief, but upbeat. Don't hold up the line.

Congratulations are customarily reserved for the groom (it was his accomplishment to win such a perfect wife). You may tell the bride she looks lovely, something you liked about the ceremony, speak God's blessings on their marriage or the like.

In some weddings, particularly Catholic ones, there will likely be a point in which the priest instructs the congregation to offer the sign of peace. This means you should stand and shake hands with the people on either side of you in the pew, saying "Peace be with you."

Funerals

Sharing another person's deepest sorrow is hard for most, but your presence at a funeral can mean a great deal to a bereaved family.

Go to the member of the family you know best and just say "I'm sorry." If there are many people present, you may not have time to say much more. If there is time, you may ask how the family is doing. Avoid clichés and platitudes like, "I'm sure you will get over it," or "It is all for the best." People should not feel that the very natural act of grieving for a loved one is not allowed and must be quickly gotten over with or that it is somehow showing a lack of faith.

RSVP

If the invitation says RSVP, which stands for the French phrase "répondez, s'il vous plaît," ("please reply"), then be courteous and reply promptly. The person who invited you wants to know if you will be coming or not; this helps them prepare for the event.

Wedding invitations often have a a card to mail back. Other invitations may have a telephone number to call. Some say "regrets only", which means that the host will count on you being there unless you tell him or her that you will not be coming.

Do not assume that anyone other than those whose names are stated on the invitation, will be welcome. Extras may overtax the venue and/or the budget.

Once you say you will come, do not change, barring an extreme emergency such as a death in the family.

© 2006 Sweet Home Press

The same guidelines apply to the "viewing" or "visitation." This is the period often set aside before the funeral. This less formal gathering affords more opportunity to interact with friends and family of the deceased. Briefly sharing a good memory about the deceased is often welcome. The family may wish to share memories of their own; be a good listener.

It is not unusual at the viewing/visitation to chat with people you know, but keep your voice subdued. Remember where you are and why you are there.

Formal Dinners

Be a good guest who adds to the value and enjoyment others get out of the gathering. Converse with those around you. Loudness, crassness, arguments and strongly stated opinions are especially inappropriate at a formal occasion. This is a time for dignified, polite conversation.

Keep things positive and light. Avoid topics that people feel strongly about, like politics, (unless you are at a political fundraiser!). This is not the time to discuss your grandmother's cancer, your aunt's divorce or other "heavy" topics. As always, avoid speaking ill of anyone.

First lady, Eleanor Roosevelt, was a frequent guest and hostess at formal dinners. She'd play a mental ABC game to help her choose topics of conversation. She would start with a topic beginning with the letter "A", for example: "Do you recall the first time you ate an artichoke and who taught you how to eat it? (pointing to the artichoke on the dinner plate) " "Are you a baseball fan?" and so forth, picking topics running through the alphabet , until she found one of interest to her conversational partner.

Whether you use Mrs. Roosevelt's device or not, you can't go wrong by showing an interest in those around you, and drawing them out with non-threatening questions and active listening. Start with neutral topics about shared experiences like jobs, gardening, food, sports and the like.

Do your part to keep an interesting conversation flowing. It is considered good manners to divide your attention about equally between your various dinner partners.

If someone talks to you while your mouth is full, polite manners dictate pointing to your closed mouth to indicate your inability to reply at the moment. When your mouth is clear, reopen the conversation before taking more food. There are several good reasons to

Advanced Conversation with Character

take small bites. Aiding the flow of conversation is one of those good reasons.

Never allow your cell phone or pager to sound at a formal occasion. Never be seen using a cell phone, from the moment you arrive until you leave. If it cannot be avoided, excuse yourself and find a secluded place or go outside.

Be sure to express thanks to the host/hostess after the event. Appropriate comments include: "You were so kind to invite me," "I had a lovely time," and "The food was delicious."

Some formal occasions will have reception lines. This is simply an efficient way for the hosts to thank their guests for coming and to 'touch base' with each person. Do not carry food or drink with you; that would make hand shaking awkward and you certainly don't want to spill something on your hosts!

Do not try to start a conversation or ask a question in the line. If you are asked a question, keep the answer as brief as politely possible ,and move quickly along to allow those following you to be greeted. After the greeting, move away; never stand around in a formal greeting area.

☑ Plan of Action

- ☐ Research proper etiquette for a formal event, like a wedding, funeral or formal dinner. Make a list of tips you learn. This need not be a real upcoming event, but it could be.

- ☐ Now learn and list tips for that event if it were held in a different culture.

- ☐ Hold a mock formal dinner in your home. Set the table, dress and act in all ways as if this were truly a formal affair.

- ☐ With your family, role play a reception line.

- ☐ To practice general dinner time conversation, play the "alphabet game" at the family dinner table, thinking of topics from "A" to "Z."

15 Other Social Occasions

> **Philippians 2:4**
>
> ...do not merely look out for your own personal interests, but also for the interests of others.

> A gift, with a kind countenance, is a double present.
>
> **Thomas Fuller**

At Friend's Homes

Some folks just seem to shine at a social occasion. For the rare person, it just seems to come naturally. Most of us have to learn "the standard social graces" the hard way—by learning and practicing.

This chapter helps you get your good social bearings on a less-than-formal occasion.

If You are the Host

Greet your guest outside or at the door. Take their coat, if they have one, and hang it up. If this is a first visit, show them around the house. Introduce them to all family members and pets in the house. Provide your guest with especially helpful information, like where they can find their coat later and in which room to find other guests. Inform young visitors of house rules, like, "Don't feed the dog," or "We aren't allowed in the bedrooms."

If you have just one or two guests and/or no pre-planned agenda, suggest a few activities and ask your guest(s) for ideas. Decide on something you will both enjoy.

If anyone is being unkind to one of your guests (like teasing), or if they are offending or embarrassing someone out of ignorance, it is your responsibility as host/hostess to put a stop to the problem. Whether you directly address the problem with the offending party privately or whether you can tactfully put a stop to the offending or talk, on the spot, is a matter

© 2006 Sweet Home Press

Advanced Conversation with Character

for your own judgment. When a young person cannot handle the matter, they should get a parent involved.

When it is time for your guest to leave, walk to the door with them. Say good-bye and that you are glad they came. Be sensitive to their time schedule. Don't keep them longer than they want and certainly don't keep a child beyond when their parent expects them home. Know when and how to end a conversation.

If You Are the Guest

Be friendly to everyone in the family. Never ignore or be unkind to younger siblings or treat your friend's parents like the maid or chauffeur, there only to do things for you. Your friend's parents will likely judge by your words and actions whether you are a suitable friend for their child.

When greeting your friend's parents, make the effort to look into their eyes with a pleasant face. Thank them for having you to their house and for courtesies like driving you home. Answer respectfully, with a "Yes" or "Yes, ma'am" rather than 'Yeah," or with just a nod and a grunt.

Before leaving, be sure to find your host and thank them for having you. If you had a good time, tell them so. Surely, there was something you enjoyed or found interesting that can make for a positive parting comment.

It's a Party!

Appropriate behavior at a party is in some ways similar to a visit with a friend and in some ways like that at a formal occasion.

Tag, You're It!

If name tags are worn, they should be placed on the right shoulder. The reason for this is that most people are right handed and when people shake hands, using their right hand, this is where the eye can best see the name tag and the name of the person.

Do not wear a nametag on your belt or lower body. This makes it awkward for people trying to learn your name, and you may find it disconcerting when people's eyes start searching your body for a name.

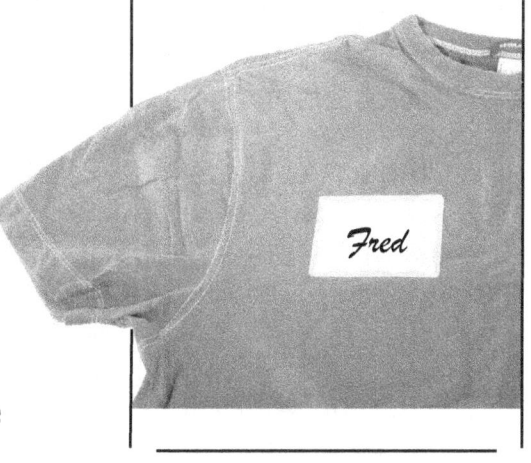

© 2006 Sweet Home Press

15 Other Social Situations

As Host or Hostess

It is your job to help everyone have a good time. Greet your guest as they arrive. A hostess will cordially greet a guest with a cheery, "I am so pleased you could come," and then get them engaged in conversation with other guests so you are free to greet other arrivals.

As guests begin to leave, make sure to say good-bye to each one and thank them for coming. Help them to remember their coats, party bags, the dish they brought or anything else they came with or need to take. If there is food leftover that a guest seemed to like, you might suggest they take some with them.

As a Guest

It is difficult to enter a room full of strangers and start a conversation, so be prepared. Before entering an event, take a couple of minutes and think of at least three conversation topics. Make a short list of things going on in your life that you'd be willing to share with others, of news items that might be of interest to people who you know will be at the party and any unusual or interesting current events.

Remind yourself of what you may already know about fellow attendees: Their hobbies, activities or interests, and recall if there is anything important going on in their life about which you should ask. If you happen to encounter an uncomfortable silence, these conversation points will come in handy.

Exude confidence with your body language, even if you are not feeling confident. Nervous habits like twisting your hair, slouching shoulders and averted eyes can make others uncomfortable, too.

Don't just stick to the people you know best. Make an effort to talk to anyone you don't know very well. Pay particular attention to guests who may not know anyone, who are alone, or who are looking ill at ease with a group of strangers.

Sometimes you will need or want to end one conversation so you can talk with someone else. Be sensitive not to hurt your conversational partner's feelings. Say something like this: "It was nice talking to you. Maybe we can talk again later," or "I think I'll get something to eat now. May I get something for you?" or "Excuse me please. I see a friend I need to talk to. I'll see you later."

At a Nursing Home

While a visit to a nursing home can bless you more than you might imagine, more than most any place, this is the occasion to be a servant who seeks nothing but the well-being of those you visit. At a party, it is time to have fun. At a nursing home, it is time

© 2006 Sweet Home Press

Advanced Conversation with Character

to focus on the needs of others.

If the person you visit is receptive, hold their hand, give them hugs when you arrive and leave, and make eye contact when they are talking to you. Many times, the only touch a resident receives is when they are dressed or bathed.

Listen attentively. Do not dominate the conversation or talk "at" the resident. Don't patronize by saying "we," as in "Did we have a good lunch?" Even if you have heard their story before, being a good listener allows them to enjoy their memories or current thoughts by sharing them with you.

It isn't as important what they say, or say over again, to you. That you are there to listen is of most import.

Share news about your life and your family. Bring a photo album. But sense at what point the nursing home resident loses interest.

Do not spend the entire visit asking questions about how they feel or if they have eaten. They may hear enough of that from the nursing home staff. Instead, share funny stories or talk about a big decision you have made. When visiting your relatives in a nursing home, tell them about trivial events, too. Even little details can be important and make elders feel included in family life.

☑ Plan of Action

- ☐ Visit a nursing home or an elderly friend or family member, and put the tips you read in this chapter into practice. Prepare ahead of time by considering stories you might tell, bringing photos, if appropriate, and the like.

- ☐ The next time you will be a guest, prepare ahead of time. Review the *As a Guest* section in this chapter, and carry out the instructions there, including:
  - Plan three conversation topics.
  - Make a list of items of interest.
  - Consider what you know is going on in the lives of others.

© 2006 Sweet Home Press

16 Political Activism

1 Timothy 2:1-4
I urge that entreaties and prayers, petitions and thanksgivings, be made on behalf of all men, for kings and all who are in authority, so that we may lead a tranquil and quiet life in all godliness and dignity.

All that is necessary for the triumph of evil is that good men do nothing.

Edmund Burke

Our daughter served as an intern with a seasoned political activist one year. She learned from her mentor that politicians are continually bombarded with letters, e-mails, phone calls and personal contact in which people are unhappy about something they've done or stood for. She learned that a word of appreciation or a simple "Thank-you for serving us" stands out like a neon light. Politicians are people too. They need to be treated with respect and kindness, even those, or maybe especially those, with whom we do not always see eye to eye.

Tactics for Tackling Legislators

1. **Be brief**
   Politicians are busy people. They want to know what your main concerns are and what can they do to help.

2. **Stick to the facts**
   This is not the time for violins and sad stories. Start with an authoritative overview, based on facts.

3. **Add in personal experiences**
   This won't be effective on its own without the facts, but can add a human element and make you stand out from the 'experts' politicians talk to often. Avoid second hand anecdotes; share from your own personal experience.

4. **Make it relevant**
   Give politicians a reason for listening to

© 2006 Sweet Home Press

you by telling them how the issue affects the electorate in their area.

5. **Include a call to action**
Be sure to tell your listener what you want them to do; what they can do to solve the problem you outlined. Be very clear about this.

6. **Be polite**
You need not be very formal. In fact, that can come across as pompous. But there is no excuse for not being courteous. Thank the politician listening to you. Politicians have a lot of demands on their time and will appreciate being thanked for making the effort.

☑ Plan of Action

☐ Bless your legislator. Send a note of thanks for their service, without asking for anything of them. Or find out their birthday by calling their office, and send them a card. In both cases, an old fashioned letter sent through the mail means more than an email. (Sending mail to public office holders has become more complicated in the era of terrorism. Ask how best to send correspondence—especially for federal legislators.)

☐ Don't forget the most important communication: Pray for those in leadership. Now that, indeed, is a *conversation with character*!

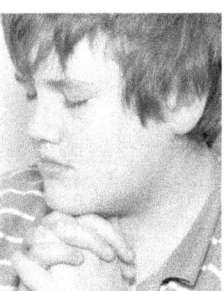

Advanced Conversation with Character

Give the Office Holder Context

I sat down for the first time with my U.S. Representative in his office to request that he support an issue. Before we got very far in the conversation, he wanted to know about me and my extended family. He was sizing up who I know and who I was connected to. He wanted to decide the political impact of how he might respond.

Those are the political facts of life, so to speak. To stay in office, it seems every politician must keep the political angle in mind.

If you know the office holder, then give them context when introducing them to others. If the person you introduce is the leader of an organization, let the officeholder know that up front.

You thereby gain the officeholder's trust.

© 2006 Sweet Home Press

17 Getting Closer

Getting closer is a risky and rewarding adventure. This chapter helps you lower the risk and increase the reward of closer friendships.

Facts

Facts are important—no denying it. If you don't know that someone was raised by wolves and prefers to gnaw on bones during a conversation, you might mistake their seeming strangeness for hostility. You might not press forward to learn their true feelings about weightier issues like gun legislation, dietary laws and the protection of endangered species. Having failed to learn such facts, you might let slip your own opinions, which would hinder their objectivity about who you really are.

So, yes, facts have their place in a conversation. They provide a reference point from which we can take the quest for getting to know each other much further.

Developing intimacy in relationships, however, requires revealing who you are, beyond the facts. This *revealing* includes sharing opinions and feelings in a way that invites the same from another person, and in a way that assures that person that you accept them, no matter what they feel or believe.

I John 1:7

If we walk in the Light as He Himself is in the Light, we have fellowship with one another...

Wishing to be friends is quick work, but friendship is a slow-ripening fruit."

Aristotle

© 2006 Sweet Home Press

Advanced Conversation with Character

Opinions

People don't REALLY get to know who you are by facts, alone. Sharing your views on politics, what makes a book "good" or "bad," or why one worldview makes more sense than another, helps people know you much better than by simply telling where you live and that you have two sisters and a brother.

Sharing opinions is one way to reveal who you are. Opinions should, however, be communicated with discretion and tact, lest you drive people away. Samuel Clements, better known by his pen name, Mark Twain, described the perils of stating opinions as absolute fact: "His answers were so final and exact that he did not leave a doubt to hang conversation on." (from *Rambling Notes of an Idle Excursion*)

Nor do we get to know others if we quickly cut them off for their stated opinions. In matters of opinion, remain open to hear other viewpoints, thoughts and ideas.

Even when a person is sure they are correct, it is helpful and respectful to try to understand the other person's point of view and to ask questions to discover why they think as they do.

Feelings

Facts provide a framework, and opinions help people get to know you better. Yet, the recipe for a deep and trusting relationship requires a third ingredient—telling how you feel. Do you find it difficult to tell about your struggles, your joys, your frustrations and your highest aspirations when no one is in the room is willing to volunteer such information? Have you experienced how others

Relationship Spoilers

Odd Man Out
In a group or conversational trio, discussing matters that don't pertain to all present leaves some feeling like the odd person out. An example is discussing family matters when the third person is not in your family. The third person then has nothing to contribute to the conversation.

Breeding Jealousy
Don't talk at length about "my best friend Sam" to another boy who would also like to think of himself as your friend and who might feel hurt that you do not consider him a 'best friend'.

Prejudging
You may think you know what a person is going to say. Give them a chance to voice their perspective, anyway. You may hear something you didn't expect. In any case, attentive listening with a respectful posture helps to preserve the friendship.

tend to "open up" and express similar feelings after someone else "breaks the ice" by sharing their feelings? Soon, those who have shared feel much closer.

Consider the following statements.

Fact Only: I saw a reading list on the internet with over 1000 book reviews.

Fact Plus Opinion: I saw a reading list on the internet with over 1000 reviews. I think it's important to have guidelines in selecting books, because books shape our minds, beliefs and decisions.

Fact Plus Opinion Plus Feelings: I saw a reading list on the internet with over 1000 reviews. I think it's important to have guidelines in selecting books, because books shape our minds, beliefs and decisions. I just love to read, and I was so excited to discover this new list because I really trust the reviewer. I can't wait to check them out!

The progression above, from fact to opinion to feelings is analogous to going from one-dimensional to two-dimensional to three-dimensional.

Disclosing feelings helps connect to others who have experienced similar feelings. Feeling lonely in a crowd, frustration over a series of obstacles to a goal, the enjoyment of a relaxing walk on a beautiful autumn day and the embarrassment over something awkward done in public are examples of situations most anyone can relate to. Instead of simply reciting facts about the class you are taking or the subjects you are taking in school, try adding interest by telling about your reactions, hopes, desires and other feelings. Remember, people are not looking for more entertainment— a funny movie or book can fill the bill there. In a conversation, they aren't usually looking just for new facts. They are looking for connection with another person. Consider this example:

Just the Facts

"I just started a new class. It's an art class and it meets on Tuesday evenings. We are starting with pencil sketching. Later we will learn about watercolor and oil painting and other media."

Adding Self Disclosure

"I've wanted to improve my art skills for ages and I'm so excited because I finally started an art class this past Tuesday night. I was kind of nervous because I really don't know if I have any talent, but I was amazed at how much improvement I saw after the teacher showed us a few tips. I love to write and always thought it would be fun to be able to illustrate my own books; maybe, just maybe, I'll be able to do that someday. This class gives me hope!"

Be Real

Everyone relates better to people willing to admit their faults and weaknesses, since we all have them. Someone who comes across too perfect can be intimidating or seem proud.

That doesn't mean that you should go around parading your faults, either; just keep a balanced picture going. If you are telling about reaching the state championships in the national spelling bee, and all the wins it took to get you there, for example, throw in a few tidbits about problems you encountered, mistakes you made, or times you were really nervous.

If you just tell people what you think they want to hear, you are portraying an unreal person. If someone likes you, it won't really be YOU they like. You'll have to keep up the 'act' and the whole relationship will be built on a false foundation

☑ Plan of Action

Samuel Clements said "Sane and intelligent human beings are like all other human beings, and carefully and cautiously and diligently conceal their private real opinions from the world and give out fictitious ones in their stead for general consumption."

☐ What do you think of that idea? Why? Why do you think Mark Twain thought people kept their private opinions to themselves and gave out false ones ? Discuss this with your family, or express your thoughts in an essay of one or more pages.

Advanced Conversation with Character

Words Are Forever

I shot an arrow into the air,

It fell to earth, I knew not where;

For so swiftly it flew, the sight

Could not follow it in its flight.

I breathed a song into the air,

It fell to earth, I knew not where;

For, who has sight so keen and strong

That it can follow the flight of song?

Long, long afterward, in an oak

I found the arrow, still unbroke;

And the song, from beginning to end,

I found again in the heart of a friend.

-Henry Wadsworth Longfellow

© 2006 Sweet Home Press

18 To Every Tribe and Tongue

Mark 16:15

And He said to them, "Go into all the world and preach the gospel to all creation."

It is the common wonder of all men, how among so many million faces, there should be none alike.

Sir Thomas Browne

When we lived in Europe, we observed with a mixture of amusement and embarrassment, American tourists who were not fluent in the native language. Attempting to overcome that barrier, they spoke louder, talked "baby talk," and/or tried speaking English with a German accent. It worked in the movies, right?

When we stumbled through our own conversations in German (not our native tongue) we felt inept and limited in our ability to communicate. We were frustrated and humiliated at seeming so ignorant.

In our own country, we tend to think the foreigner speaking to us in broken English is not very bright, since he or she seems to be talking like a child, stumbling and making errors. The truth is, for most people, learning a new language is difficult. The person who does so may sound ignorant in their imperfect speech, but they are probably very bright, indeed.

In many countries, as many as a dozen or 100 or more languages are commonly spoken. Europeans routinely travel across national borders as Americans travel from U.S. state to state. Most of the world's inhabitants are expected to understand other languages and cultures. As the song goes, "It's A Small World, After All."

This chapter helps you understand and effectively communicate with people whose first language is not your own. An important precursor to effective conversation is an understanding of cultural differences.

© 2006 Sweet Home Press

Advanced Conversation with Character

General Tips

While there are specifics for each culture, there are some general tips for speaking to people from a different culture.

Be Friendly, but Not Too Friendly

Americans tend to talk too much, share facts, opinions and feelings more openly and send out "let's be friends" signals more readily than in other cultures. A more reserved conversational style is safer and more appropriate.

Beware of Gestures

It is best to avoid hand gestures and other physical signals until you know a culture well. The customary "ok" sign, the thumbs-up, beckoning with one's hand, standing with hands in pockets or raising an open hand to refuse something, to name a few examples, can have very different meanings in other cultures. Sometimes, those meanings are rude or crude. Other times, they are simply unfamiliar to the other person.

In India, for example, wagging of the head side-to-side might mean "Yes" or any number of other things. It does not mean "No."

Punctuality is Relative to Culture

Time awareness varies greatly from culture to culture. It is generally safe to arrive on time; at worst, you may surprise the person you are meeting. If the other person arrives significantly later than the scheduled time, don't be offended or angry. This is quite normal in a number of cultures.

When "Funny" Seems "Strange"

Mark Twain once said, "Guides cannot master the subtleties of the American joke." What is regarded as funny differs from

---

Let your "Yes" be "Yes," or Was that a "No?"

In Bulgaria and Greece an upward nod of the head means "No," while tilting the head side-to-side means "Yes."

Even if your foreign friend is capable and kind enough to speak to you in English, don't get caught off guard when their head movements speak another language.

When Pounds Are Not Measured in Pounds.

An American told of his experience ordering a sandwich in London, England. "How much is that sandwich," our friend inquired. One pound, responded the shopkeeper. "No," clarified our friend, "I don't want to know how much it weighs, I want to know how much it costs."

This time, the shopkeeper emphatically assured him that the sandwich cost "one pound!"

You see, the British unit of money is called the pound, not he dollar.

culture to culture, and much of American humor does not translate well.

In Mexico, our daughter found that sarcasm is not considered humorous.

Americans use sarcastic comments in good-natured "ribbing." For instance, we might say to a forgetful person, "Don't forget to take your head with you." Some cultures take such comments literally. They don't understand the humor (or even that humor is intended), and they may be offended.

On the other hand, our Australian friends tell us that the use of sarcasm is even more common in their culture than in the United States.

In any case, Americans turn to humor all too easily for many cultures. We use humor to communicate friendliness, to put others at ease or in reaction to our own sense of insecurity. In general, Americans do well to resist the frequent temptation to resort to humor when around people from other cultures.

Saving Face

"Saving face" is important to people in Eastern cultures. When you help a person conceal an offense, you are helping them "save face," avoiding their embarrassment. For instance, you may arrive at a Filipino home for a party and find that your guest is running out of food. You help your host save face by indicating that you are not hungry, that you ate before you came or by saying something truthful that provides the host a way out of the predicament.

As feared as public embarrassment is to people in any culture, it is especially catastrophic in some. Be sensitive to recognize when this could be a problem, and stand ready to help save face.

Watch Those Feet

In many countries, it is customary to remove your shoes before entering a home. Try to observe what others do and follow their lead if you are unsure. Offenses in some cultures include pointing feet towards another person or showing the bottoms of feet.

Personal Space

How close is too close to another person? In predominantly United States culture, comfortable distance between people engaged in a conversation is at least two foot lengths. In some South American countries, this space is about one foot length. People who live in densely populated areas are accustomed to closer spaces.

Eye Contact

In America, if we don't make eye contact we are perceived as evasive, dishonest or embarrassed. In some cultures, direct eye contact

© 2006 Sweet Home Press

Advanced Conversation with Character

is seen as aggressive and intimidating. In some cultures, direct eye contact from female to male is considered very forward.

When All Else Fails

A little study of the culture in advance of contact can save a lot of miscommunication. If that is not possible, at least understand the various ways your own personal habits might cause problems outside of your own culture. You can't know everything, and people are generally understanding of cultural errors, but they appreciate attempts to be sensitive.

And, lest we forget to say: People are individuals and defy stereotype.

Starting Places

When you encounter someone from another culture, you may need an icebreaker or two to get two-way conversation flowing. Ask questions about where the person lives (or where they came from). For example, "Tell me about the town you came from." or "Please teach me how to say please and thank-you in your language." (Or, "Yes" and "No," etc.)

Remember these basic expressions and use them the next time you meet. This will help your new friend to feel that you value and respect their culture.

Love Is Not Easily Offended

In addition to not innocently offending others, neither be easily offended *by others*. Your new friend may find it quite natural to ask you how much you paid for your house or what you earn on your job. Being three hours late for an appointment may be the norm where they come from. Avoiding eye

Let's Do the International Two-Step!

This can be fun. Imagine that someone from rural England (where personal space is wide) meets a Middle Easterner (where personal space is closer). The Middle Easterner steps forward to engage the conversation. The Englander steps back. The Middle Easterner steps forward. The Englishman, who is now against the wall, takes two steps to the side. The Middle Easterner takes one step forward and one to the side. Add some music, and you have a new International dance. It goes on all

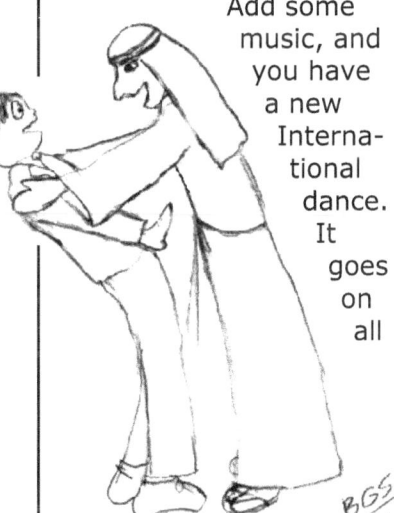

over the world. The morale of the story is, if you find your conversation "has legs," be willing to sacrifice a few inches of personal space to aid communication.

© 2006 Sweet Home Press

18 Every Tribe and Tongue

contact may be a sign of respect. Don't allow such unexpected turns in a conversation to shut down your communication.

We had a little joke among fellow missionaries working with refugees from many lands. We were trained to say to ourselves, "It is not wrong, it is just 'cultural'." Yet, sometimes, everything inside us wanted to scream, "It isn't cultural, it is just wrong!"

Even if you think it, try not to act it.

Travel Abroad

Even if we American's love America and feel we have something here that is special, remember that people in other lands have warm feelings for their homeland, as well. Just as we expect foreign visitors to be respectful of our country while they are here, we should expect the same of ourselves when we are the foreigner.

Attitudes to Leave at Home

As the nation with the strongest economy, strongest military and a flood of movies and music popularly embraced around the world, we Americans take attitudes with us to other lands that should be left at home. Those attitudes proceed from the mouth in some ugly ways. For instance:

"Why don't they speak English?"

They don't need to speak English. They need to speak the language of their own country. You are the visitor, so at least make an attempt to learn a few phrases in the their language, and don't assume everyone in the world should learn yours.

Then there are the negative comments:

"Everything is so dirty here, and the food is nasty."

And negative comparisons with the United States

"Well, in America, we do it like this, and it works much better," or *"Can you believe that long black dress? Why don't they just wear jeans and a T-shirt?"*

Be Sensitive

Be sensitive to local standards of modesty. Look around and see how people dress. Are women wearing pants? Shorts? Loose clothing? Skirts below the knees? Jewelry? Simple observation will save you from causing inadvertent offense. You probably don't realize how bizarre your own sense of "appropriate" attire looks to other people.

© 2006 Sweet Home Press

Advanced Conversation with Character

☑ Plan of Action

☐ Think about who you will come in contact with this week from a different culture. Maybe you don't expect to see any "foreigners" in your town. What about "those northerners," or "those southerners?" What about cultures in your community that vary along racial lines? Study that culture. Make a list of differences. Consider how your own habits might derail effective communication. Many excellent web sites and books found at most large library systems will help you.

Other ways to learn include eating at a restaurant serving *genuine* food from another culture. (You won't learn much about Mexico at Taco Bell nor about German culture by eating a "Hamburger" at McDonalds). Visit a cultural event, like festivals, fine arts displays or music performances.

If you are really serious about understanding other cultures, there is nothing like immersion into that culture—actually living there. A lesser alternative is *travel* to another land. You may have only enough time to learn from mistakes but the learning will be well worth the trip. While travel is costly, when weighed against one semester of college tuition, a trip abroad is one of the greatest educational bargains there is.

Short of traveling halfway around the world, some people study other cultures by volunteering to teach English to immigrants or by learning a foreign language. Be ready and willing to "go into all the world," even if, for you, that means befriending the *strange* culture in your town.

Divided by a Common Language

When we lived in England, after several years in German-speaking Austria, we breathed a sigh of relief that we would be able to understand the local language, and that the English would understand us. We knew, of course, that there were challenges understanding accents. But we looked forward to making our new home in a place that made cultural sense to us.

What we failed to fully realize was that the English are no more like Americans than Austrians. They have a distinct culture, with many opportunities for us to unknowingly damage relationships—and, looking back, it seems we took advantage of many such opportunities.

There is a saying that the Americans and British are a people "divided by a common language." Culturally, we are not as close as we may sound. It takes work to understand each other.

© 2006 Sweet Home Press

19 Silence is Golden

Ecclesiastes 3:1, 7

There is an appointed time for everything. And there is a time for every event under heaven—A time to be silent and a time to speak.

It is the province of knowledge to speak and it is the privilege of wisdom to listen.

Oliver Wendell Holmes

Silence is golden—ask any mother of young children. Do you remember how your parent(s) used to keep you from talking too much? It was for good reason. Now that you are older, knowing when to talk and when to remain silent is an important key to relationships and success.

This chapter teaches when to keep quiet and why. As the saying goes, "Silence speaks for itself."

Times NOT to Talk

Wondering when to talk and when to not talk? Most people can figure out when, but here is when not.

1. When you have food in your mouth. Gelett Burgess sums this up in his description of the dreadful Goops:
   *The Goops they talk while eating,
   And loud and fast they chew;
   And that is why I'm glad that I
   Am not a Goop—are you?*

2. During a wedding, concert, movie or anytime talk would distract others.

3. When you have something bad to say about someone. "Speak not evil one of another, brethren" - James 4:11

4. During times of silent prayer or meditation.

5. When you should be listening!

These are just to get you started. Write down other times in your life that call for

© 2006 Sweet Home Press

> **Advanced Conversation with Character**

silence. If you run short of ideas, ask a parent, and take plenty of paper with you.

Listen Actively

The listening part of a conversation is not merely absence of talking. Listening takes real effort. If you are not certain you understand, say back to the other person what you think they mean. This helps to avoid misunderstandings and it shows that you want to understand.

Listen for More Than Facts

Sometimes what you are listening for is not information as much as opinions and emotions. In such cases, ask yourself what the other person is feeling and what message they are trying to get across, as in these examples:

Friend: I'll never make the team

You: You are feeling frustrated, aren't you?

Friend: Yeah. Every time the coach is watching, I make some big goof. He must think I am hopeless!

You: Do you feel he isn't getting a realistic picture of you as a ball player?

Friend: Exactly! He just always seems to be watching at my worst moments!

—

Mom: Turn that radio down!

You: Are you mad at me?

Mom: No, I am just trying to concentrate on this letter I am writing, and it's hard to think with the music playing so loud.

A Self Check

Check your listening skills with the following questions. Think about each question before answering, and be honest with yourself. Circle your answer to each question.

1. I listen to a person first, and then I decide on the importance of what is being said:

    Usually? or Seldom?

2. I put aside what I am doing, ignoring distractions, so I can pay full attention.

    Usually? or Seldom?

3. I show interest and respect to the person speaking. I don't just *pretend* to be interested.

    Usually? or Seldom?

4. I listen, without interrupting , even if I think I already know what the person will say.

    Usually? or Seldom?

(continued, next page)

© 2006 Sweet Home Press

19 Silence is Golden

A Self Check, continued

5. I listen equally well to different people, young and old, men and women, people of different races, rich and poor just the same.

    Usually? or Seldom?

6. I make eye contact with the person speaking.

    Usually? or Seldom?

7. I really try to understand what the person is telling me and how they feel about it, rather than just defending my own point of view.

    Usually? or Seldom?

8. I avoid a debate mentality, in which proving myself right is more important than understanding another person.

    Usually? or Seldom?

9. I don't let telephones or other distractions in the room interrupt my listening or interrupt what another person is trying to say.

    Usually? or Seldom?

How did you do? Make note of any weaknesses, and work on improvement.

In both of these exchanges, it was more important to understand the feelings and intentions than to gather information.

Listening Conveys Acceptance

Rather than telling a person right off what they SHOULD be doing or feeling, or just expressing sympathy or reassurance, help them feel that their problems are understood and that you have confidence in their ability to handle them.

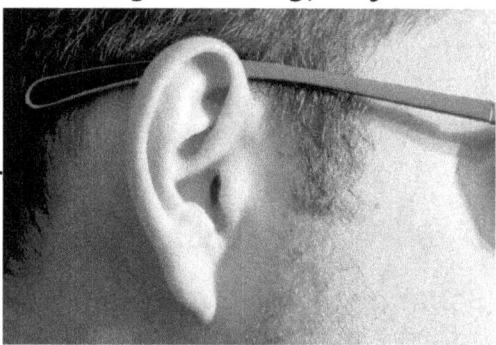

Actively listening, rather than judging, preaching or criticizing, helps deepen relationships and encourages more confidences, We all need acceptance of our thoughts and feelings.

Consider Context

Active listening does *not* mean just repeating or paraphrasing what was said, as in:

"I feel sick"

"Oh, you don't feel well?"

Better to ask about symptoms, how long they have felt that way and/or how you can help.

You can learn even more by observing body language and facial expression. When they say, "I feel sick." consider the tone of voice and the context of the statement. Are they saying they are about to throw up or that this feeling came over them suddenly? Or, are they simply reaffirming a long-standing condition?

Is this perhaps not a physical sickness, but an emotional reaction to a bad situation? The active listener learns so much more than mere words convey.

☑ Plan of Action

- ☐ Drawing from the Self Check list and the undesirable gestures in the list to the right, identify two or three ways you need to improve your listening. Write them down. Look at the list each morning to remind yourself. Make a conscious effort this week to improve your listening. Meal times with family are a great place to start.

- ☐ In the chapter, *Getting Closer*, we discussed the *facts*, *opinions* and *feelings* parts of a conversation. Listen to a conversation in which you are not an active participant. Note how many facts, opinions and feelings are expressed. This non-participant listening practice will sharpen your listening skills for when you are an active listener.

> **Advanced Conversation with Character**
>
> **Keep Your Body In Check When Listening**
>
> When listening, remain aware of your posture and gestures. Your mouth might be silent, but your body might be sending all kinds of messages. Guard against gestures that indicate you not interested, you are bored, you aren't really open to the other person's ideas or that you don't take the person seriously.
>
> Guard against:
> - Doodling
> - Sighing
> - Slouching
> - Yawning
> - Looking at your watch
> - Looking over the speaker's shoulder
> - Crossing arms over your chest
> - Standing with hands on hips

20 Conversation Do's and Don'ts

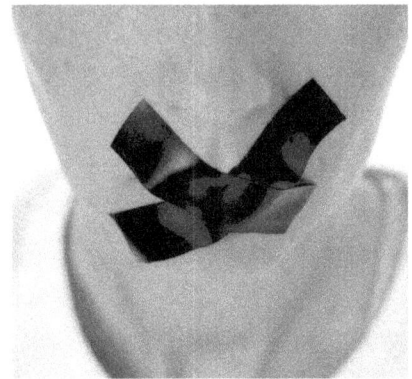

> Philippians 2:14
>
> Do all things without grumbling or disputing.

> The best way to be boring is to leave nothing out.
>
> Voltaire

This chapter will not take you a whole week to study, but it might take a long time for the advice here to soak into your mind and become a part of your actions. Read through the following list of do's and don'ts twice—once on one day, and again on another day. You will have a lifetime to apply the lessons.

Do keep conversation topics appealing to all. Some people are too squeamish to discuss operations, illnesses, dissections, the animal your dog just killed and the like, especially at the dinner table.

Don't unload your personal problems on people you hardly know: save this for your close friends.

Do maintain a balanced conversation. Of course you will share some personal experiences and ideas, but "I" in every sentence is the sure sign of a bore. (refer to *Keep an "I" Out* in book 1) A good conversation consists of balanced give and take.

Don't hype your joke or story by saying something like "This story is really hilarious". Let the audience decide that for themselves.

Do be loyal to friends and family. Referring to embarrassing mistakes they made is off limits

Don't brag or whine.

© 2006 Sweet Home Press

Advanced Conversation with Character

Do maintain a positive attitude; people will want to be around you more than if you are a complainer.

Don't pretend to know something that you don't; humility is delightful.

Do be realistic; don't expect perfection from others….or yourself!

Don't exhort those with speech impediments to 'take your time'. Don't freeze, or lose eye contact. Don't finish phrases or sentences; allow them time to complete their thoughts. Be patient and concentrate on what is being said and not how it is said.

Do be patient and respectful. It's rude to finish people's sentences for them even if you think you know what they are going to say.

Don't point or stare.

Do respect people's privacy by avoiding listening in on conversations you are not a part of.

Don't interrupt.

Do avoid personal questions such as how much things cost or why someone looks or dresses the way they do

Don't bore everyone to tears with minor details, i.e. "My grandmother went on a trip once to New Orleans, or was it Newport? Oh, I remember, it was actually New York." If it isn't truly important, get on with what you are saying.

Do speak clearly. It is annoying to have to continually ask someone to repeat themselves or to guess at what was said.

Ten Commandments for Conversation with Character

1. Do make God's word the final word.
2. Don't be over-impressed by your own words.
3. Do not make wrongful use of the name of the Lord your God.
4. Do rest from talking.
5. Do speak to your parents with respect and honor.
6. Do not kill people with your words.
7. Do not steal your neighbor's joy or self-respect.
8. Do not take and use your neighbor's words as your own.
9. Do not lie about your neighbor.
10. Do not covet your neighbor's gift of speech.

© 2006 Sweet Home Press

Don't insult people, directly or indirectly. Examples of indirect insults would be: "I don't care if other people say you're boring (or ugly or opinionated etc.)", " Even you could understand this." and "Well, I'd like to tell you about that but I don't think you'd be able to understand."

Cell Phone Do's and Don'ts

Do turn the ringer off during a meeting or interview and don't answer any calls.

Don't talk in elevators, libraries, class, museums, restaurants, theaters, dentist or doctor waiting rooms, places of worship, while in a check out line or working in one, auditoriums or other enclosed public spaces, such as hospital emergency rooms or buses.

Do maintain at least a 10-foot zone from anyone while talking

Don't have any loud or emotional conversations in public .

Do give conversational partners your full attention. Don't answer or make any calls that are not urgent.

Don't talk and eat at the same time. Yuck!

Tips On Netiquette

If your family does not use the internet, or if you have internet access in your home, but are not free to engage in all of the communication options found there, then you are not alone. The internet is a dangerous place. It can be like a stroll at night through the worst part of a big city.

Sooner or later, however, you will probably depend on the internet for communication more than you now do.

A great deal of conversation takes place over the internet. As of this writing, the two most common ways people converse electronically, other than through email (discussed in another chapter), is on forums and chats.

Forums

A forum is a place on the internet where people with a common interest post messages. For instance, a forum might be for people who grow fruit trees. A member will start a topic, often in the form of a question, like, "When should I trim my trees?" Other members will see the question and send their ideas on when trees should be trimmed. The thread of messages,

© 2006 Sweet Home Press

including responses back and forth between members, is like a slow-motion conversation. Some responses may not come for days.

Chat

Faster paced online conversation takes place in a "chat room." Similar to a forum, people with common interests send messages back and forth in rapid succession, just as if they were talking on the telephone. Unlike a forum, the

conversation is normally not posted on the internet for all the world to read.

Chat and Forum Netiquette

"What is netiquette?" you might ask. Take off the "n," and what do you have? *Etiquette.* Netiquette is etiquette on the net, or internet. Here is a sampling of netiquette tips:

- Do read the rules for the forum or chat room you join.
- Don't use your real name, for your own safety. In most cases, it is acceptable to use a pseudonym to protect your privacy. It is not being dishonest; it is expected.
- Don't provide personal details about yourself or where you live, as a precaution against untrustworthy people,
- Do briefly introduce yourself in a way that tells other members about your interest in the general topic (like fruit trees).
- Do search for previous discussions on forums before starting a new topic with a question that was answered earlier.
- Do read the comments posted on a particular topic before jumping in with your own ideas or questions. Otherwise, you may end up interrupting the conversation and embarrassing yourself.

If, or when, you become involved in forums or chats, you can find plenty more tips online.

☑ Plan of Action

☐ The only suggested plan of action for this chapter is that you read the do's and don'ts list twice, and that you start using them as a guide in conversations.

Advanced Conversation with Character

21 Parting Thoughts

Proverbs 10:19
When there are many words, transgression is unavoidable, but he who restrains his lips is wise.

If you want a happy ending, that depends, of course, on where you stop your story.

Orson Welles

Did you ever hear a recording, like a CD or an old style record, that keeps playing the same line over and over again. It is not unlike a conversation that doesn't know how to end.

This chapter provides tips for bringing a conversation to a successful conclusion.

Positive Ways to Close a Conversation

Even the most delightful conversations must come to an end. This unfortunate fact is discussed in the book of basics, **Conversation with Character**. Sometimes conversational partners become uncomfortable during a brief period of silence, and the conversation abruptly ends. How much better to end in a way that leaves everyone feeling good about the time just spent together.

Maybe it is time for you to go, or you feel it is time to close the conversation. Use the active listening skills you learned earlier to detect a natural break in the current topic. This pause provides the opportunity to move the conversation gracefully to a close. Here are some ways to do that:

- Briefly summarize the other person's main point(s), indicating that you hear and understand, and that there is little more they need to add. This also shows that you were listening.

© 2006 Sweet Home Press

Advanced Conversation with Character

- Make a closing comment like this: "You have some good ideas. I'll try that and let you know how it works for me."

- If your conversation included planning for something in the future, say something like, "Okay, I will get the information you need and get back to you next week," or "I really look forward to see you at the party."

- If the other person shared some challenge in life or their hopes and dreams, if appropriate say "I'll be praying for you about _____; let me know how it goes." (Be sure to actually pray.)

- Make a friendly remark, and use the person's name: "I really enjoyed talking with you, David."

Every situation may require a slightly different tact. There will be a few more parting comments, but your attempt will have failed if the other person launches back into the same topic at length or if they introduce an entirely new topic. As soon as possible, smile, make eye contact, and then leave. Avoid long, drawn-out good-byes.

Keep Bridges Open

Only in war does one burn bridges, and, even then, it can be a mistake. An ancient Chinese principle of war suggests that, after troops cross a body of water to conquer a city, boats and bridges should be burned to show the people that the invading army has no plans to leave.

Folklore has it that the French general, Napoleon, once burned bridges behind the army to discourage defections in the face of the battle ahead. More typically, in war, a retreating army will burn a bridge to hold off the advancing enemy. This is what

---

Forever Good-Byes

Some good-byes are forever—at least "forever" in this life. Words tend to fail us when we face a loved one for the last time. The scene may be in an airport, in a church parking lot, at a graduation ceremony or in a hospital. When we know this may be the "last good-bye," parting words are like the final notes in a symphony.

Partings are a fitting time to

- Affirm what is good in a person.
- Warn them of peril, if needed.
- Assure them of your love.
- Express confidence in their future as they follow God.
- Speak blessings.

A powerful blessing, one that has been echoed through the ages, is found in the words God instructed Moses to offer to Aaron, the high priest, and his sons so that they may bless Israel. Read Numbers, chapter 6, verses 22-26.

people sometimes do in conversation, when anger or impatience takes control.

Some generals have regretted their decision to burn a bridge they thought their soldiers would never again need to cross. Likewise, an employee speaks in anger to an employer on his way out the door. A church member, a fellow motorist on the highway or neighbor does likewise.

The heat of harsh words clouds judgment, making it difficult to weigh the future impact of parting on bad terms.

If not for the sake of what is right and good, then for your own sake, leave your bridges open. Even when you think you will never see that annoying person again, or that you will never need their help, you may very well be mistaken. The world has a limited number of continents to run to. Eventually, you may again deal with the person you told to "get lost!"

As for your part, make your parting in peace.

☑ Plan of Action

- ☐ Who in your life has a hard time ending a conversation? What strategies or phrases can you use in your next conversation with them to bring the conversation to a conclusion at the right time and without damaging relations? Write down those ideas.

- ☐ Find examples of how people in the Bible said farewells. Note the blessings and encouragement often imparted.

- ☐ Think of someone dear to you who might be leaving. Or, perhaps you are the one who might be leaving them. Maybe you anticipate that an older sibling will one day marry and move away.

What would you say to that person when you part? Review the tips under "Forever Good-Byes" to aid your thinking.

© 2006 Sweet Home Press